CONSULTING SUCCESS

CONSULTING SUCCESS

The Proven Guide to Start, Run and Grow a Successful Consulting Business

Michael Zipursky

If you would like further information about Consulting Success or any of our products, programs or services please email **info@consultingsuccess.com**

Library and Archives Canada Cataloguing in Publication. Zipursky, Michael, author Consulting Success/Michael Zipursky ISBN 978-1-7750411-1-5

1. Consulting 2. Marketing. 3. Entrepreneurship

To my parents, who showed me what true love and kindness are.

Consulting Success

Table of Contents

Consulting Success

Consulting Success

Consulting Success

CHAPTER 1:

THE TRUTH ABOUT CONSULTING

What It's Really Like Being a Consultant

Consulting can be one of the greatest and most lucrative professions in the world. The more you put into it, the harder you work. And the greater the skills you develop, the more you'll get out of it, the more successful you'll become, and the more money you'll make.

There are so many aspects that make being a consultant great.

1. Flexibility

You completely control your schedule. I take time off when I want, and I can get up at any time I choose. My schedule is whatever I choose to make it.

One big myth about consulting that you'll hear from many people is that you can enjoy this kind of flexibility from day one. The people who suggest this are only telling you part of the story. While you do have complete control of when you work, in reality, if you want to succeed in this business, it takes consistent and focused effort.

Even though I can now take time off to visit with an out-of-town guest or go on a holiday whenever I choose, it took time to build my business to get to this point. While at times I have structured my schedule to work three weeks a month, taking one week off, I could only do this because I worked full-out for those three weeks.

I am also free to travel the world to work with clients. This year alone, I've spent three months in Japan and six weeks in Europe, as well as time in California, Toronto, and Mexico.

To be clear, there's huge room for flexibility when you're in control of your own schedule, but it requires a lot of hard work. Not to worry, though. In this book, you'll learn all the skills, tips, and strategies you need to get to that level of success quicker.

2. Pick and Choose Who You Want to Work With

We've all had the pleasure of working with people whose company we don't enjoy. They're annoying. They make promises and don't follow through on them. The list goes on and on. Maybe it was your boss or another employee. Whatever the case, when you're a consultant, you choose who you work with. You take on projects that interest you, that you want to work on, and you don't worry about the rest.

There is plenty of room in most consulting markets for you to pick and choose what you work on. I'll share more on that later in the book.

3. You Control Your Income Potential

There's only one person who controls what you earn, and that's you! I'm not hyping this up to sound good. You really can earn as much or as little as you want in this business.

If you want to make $80,000 to $100,000 working part-time, or $500,000 to $1 million or more a year, as a consultant, you have the ability to do this. Of course, you shouldn't expect to reach that level overnight. I'm not offering any get-rich-quick schemes or a path to instant wealth. The consulting business requires hard work, motivation, and determination on your part, but genuine success is achievable. I know because I've been doing it for many years.

The Challenges You'll Face

While consultants enjoy many advantages, they also face some difficult situations. My goal with this book is to arm you with the tools, strategies, and knowledge you need to deal with every challenge you'll encounter.

Let's take a look at some of the common challenges.

1. Loneliness, Determination, and Motivation

This may sound like an insignificant challenge. You might think, "That's not a problem for me," and you may be right. But until you dedicate all your time to becoming a consultant, you'll never know how prepared you are for these challenges.

The fact is, most consultants work alone, many from a home office. I actually recommend using a home office, but we'll discuss that later. However, when you spend a lot of time working by yourself, you must be ready for what comes with the territory.

You will feel lonely at times, so be prepared. You'll find yourself sitting in your office, staring at your computer or a piece of paper, with no one to talk to.

You'll have distractions all around you—from your TV, to surfing the web, to whatever else you can find to take your mind away from your work.

One of the greatest characteristics that a consultant can possess is motivation. You must be able to motivate yourself because, without a doubt, you will question why you're doing what you're doing. You'll ask yourself if you really should be in this position where you have no stable income, have to constantly deal with clients, and have no one to talk to regularly throughout the day.

It's not easy, but when you accept this as a normal feeling that you WILL encounter, you're halfway there.

You see, most people give up when they have this feeling and never really become consultants. They dip their toe in the water, but as soon as they feel the icy chill, they run away. That's not how you reach success.

I often find it helps to just get out. Set as many meetings with clients or prospective clients as possible. Schedule meetings with other consultants in your city. Getting out and talking with others usually restores your motivation and brings back the drive to succeed.

The key to staying motivated during times of uncertainty starts by asking yourself one critical question that not enough of us ask ourselves: "What are you great at?"

While you might find this question simplistic, I assure you it's extremely powerful. Each of us has a strength, some area in which we excel, whether it's a natural ability or one that we've developed over time.

At some point in your life, you'll find yourself (if you haven't already) searching for your passion. Wondering about your purpose on the earth. Thinking about your next step. Wanting to become more successful.

At times like that, ask yourself, "What am I really great at?" Allow me to offer you some suggestions that will help you answer that question.

Answer the following:

- When do you feel most passionate or excited?

- What does the environment around you look like when you feel happiest?

- What do friends, family, and colleagues praise you for?

- What do people always ask for your advice about?

Over the last decade, I've learned that I'm a great educator. I feel honored and satisfied when I work with clients and coach business owners and consultants.

The first time I gave a presentation to other business owners, I felt nervous. Though I had some confidence, I had a serious case of the jitters. After the presentation, however, I felt only elation. Not only did the participants come up and ask me questions, but the organizers of the event said it was a hit.

That made me feel good. I made money that day, but it wasn't about the money. Giving back to others and sharing my experiences was a wonderful experience.

It's not always easy to figure out what you're really great at, but only you can decide what is right for you. You owe it to yourself to at least entertain the idea of doing what you feel passionate about, even if it might make your life more difficult in the beginning. It's worth your time. It's your life, and you only get to live it once. Make it count.

Once you figure out what you're great at, you'll feel more purpose and more energy. When you spend more of your time working in an area that you're great at, not only will you be happier, but you'll also become more successful.

Keep yourself motivated. Create goals and work toward them. That's how you'll start making it in this business.

2. Clients, Oh My Clients!

You can't avoid dealing with client problems. Even if you pick your clients very carefully and only take on projects that you're interested in, there will still be times when things go wrong.

Client problems usually happen when you least expect them, so they can be a shock to your system. Maybe the work you thought would improve your client's business hasn't done so, and they want answers. Or maybe the payment you were supposed to receive hasn't arrived, and you're starting to worry.

You're bound to make mistakes from time to time, and when it happens, you have to find a way to correct them and make sure your client stays happy.

Expect client issues, and don't get down on yourself. They might feel like a punch in the stomach, and you might find yourself wondering if you're in the right business. Consulting can feel like riding a roller coaster sometimes, with many ups and down.

So, what helps? Always be honest with yourself and your clients. Understand that when these challenges arise, it's better to deal with them right away rather than hiding and hoping they'll go away on their own.

Enjoy the business when things are going well. When they aren't, recognize that it's just part of the cycle. Work on improving the problem, and you'll get back to the good times soon enough.

Yes, the bad days feel horrible, and often the good days just feel ordinary. But the days when you score a big contract or get a big "thank you" from a client are wonderful. They make it all worthwhile.

3. Learn, Learn, and Learn Some More

One of the keys to successful marketing and developing a thriving consulting practice is to constantly be learning.

The best and most experienced marketers don't sit at the beach all day, content and comfortable that they know everything. On the contrary, they are well aware that they don't know it all.

They shell out their hard-earned money to continue learning. They attend seminars, purchase books, try out new technologies, and pay thousands of dollars to work with coaches.

I can't tell you how important it is to read more. As you work to establish your business, you may find you have less time to pick up books and learn. I know; I've been there.

I resolved to change that, and so should you. I decided I would always MAKE time to read, and that's what I've done. I usually have several books in front of me, on subjects ranging from business, marketing, and economics to psychology, creativity, sales, and fitness.

Every time you pick up a book, you find yourself thinking of new ideas for your own business and life. You learn new things, become more knowledgeable, stimulate your mind, and get exposed to experiences, cultures, thoughts, and ideas that you otherwise might never learn about.

The most successful people in the world read. The majority of them read A LOT. Some of the most successful people I know read at least two books a month. That's twenty-four books a year. And that is what I do now.

As Mark Twain said, "The man who does not read good books has no advantage over the man who cannot read them."

The moment you stop learning is the moment you start to decline, not just mentally or physically, but financially, because your competition continues to learn. They gain the advantages you once had. Soon, they'll knock you off your comfortable position, and you'll be left trying to catch up.

Learning without implementing gives you book smarts.

Implementing without learning means you'll get a lot done, but there's a good chance you'll be doing the wrong stuff, and you'll waste a lot of time and money along the way.

Implementing as you learn on an ongoing basis is an extremely powerful combination.

4. Making Your Best Investment

You can make a stable income as a consultant. The idea that working a 9-to-5 job is more stable than being a consultant is largely a myth.

Sure, there's some truth to it. For example, working as a regular employee gives you all of the medical and insurance benefits you won't get as a consultant. Then again, as people have learned in tough economic times, your job as a regular employee isn't always as safe and secure as you think. You can be laid off, downsized, or made redundant at any time.

However, you won't get something for nothing when it comes to earning a stable income with consulting. You need to consider a few truths about consulting to give yourself the best chance of success.

First, it's important to realize that you will have some start-up costs for equipment, marketing, and promotion, which all businesses need in the early stages. These things require money, but you should look at them as a smart investment.

Not long ago, I sat down with my financial advisor to review each part of my portfolio: stocks, bonds, mutual funds, hedge funds, cash, and all the other good stuff.

I had put money into another business, but I was considering placing it into a holding account for the new business I was launching. I wanted to do this partly for protection, a buffer against any rough spots the new startup would face, but also for marketing and promotion.

Doing this would've meant I was contributing less to my investments, so I expected him to talk me out of it, to try to convince me to invest in the markets instead.

He didn't. Immediately, he said, "A business is the best investment you can make."

That has been my experience over the years, so I was happy to hear him say it. While investing in your own business can often present risks, the huge growth potential you get makes it worthwhile.

Investing $10,000 and getting $20,000, $30,000 or $50,000 in return after a few years would be considered exceptional, but when you start a consulting business, it's not uncommon to make $80,000, $100,000, even $200,000 in the first year or two.

In no way am I suggesting that you take your life savings and drop it all into starting a new business. However, investing in yourself is often the smartest investment you can make, and it offers the highest potential return.

Once you make the start-up investment, you need to consider who's going to pay you. As a consultant, you control how many clients you work with at any particular time. Some work with only one a year, others work with ten or more. Having multiple clients provides protection, so even if one of them leaves, you still have income from the others.

Now, I can imagine what you're thinking. "Yeah, but having multiple clients to work with all the time is hard." It's only hard if you structure your consulting business the wrong way.

Consulting Success

In order to keep your consulting income stable, you have to set up ongoing work with your clients. That way, your projects aren't limited to a day, week, or month.

I've used this structure successfully for years. In the Fees and Pricing chapter of this book, I'll go into detail about how you can make this work for you.

It's a great feeling to have ongoing and consistent income from consulting projects, and I'll show you how to do it.

A Day in the Life of a Consultant

Everyone has a different schedule, so I can't tell you specifically how to schedule your time. What I will share with you is my typical day as someone running a consulting business for more than 18 years.

My schedule has changed a bit since I started. The biggest shift occurred when my daughter was born. At that time, I decided to work less in order to be there for her. I wanted to ensure she saw me as a father who was present. That's a choice I made and was able to make because of the flexibility of my business.

In the early years of my business, I tended to wake up between 5:30 and 6 am every day, and then I'd work until 9 or 10 at night. You don't have to do that, and I don't recommend it. There's no good reason to kill yourself with work or neglect your family. However, I will say this: in the early stages of your business, the more focus and commitment you make, the more momentum you will generate. Getting traction in the early stages can be tough, so you can't afford to be too laid back or complacent.

As you make progress and build your business, you will reach a tipping point where a lot of good things start to happen. At that point, you can change your schedule. You won't need to chase as many clients because you'll be getting more referrals.

Here's what my schedule looked like in the early years. After waking up by 6 am, I'd go into the living room to do some morning stretches. When you sit down and work on a computer for much of the day, it's important to keep your body in good shape, and stretching is one key.

Next, I would have breakfast with my wife, read a magazine I subscribe to, or check the global news headlines. Then, I'd get on my computer, checking and replying to emails. I'd also read several blogs and other sources of industry information to make sure I was up to date.

The phone didn't usually start ringing until 9:30 or 10 am, so in these initial few hours, I tended to get a lot of work done.

By this time, I'd showered and freshened up. On some days, I'd schedule 10 am meetings with clients, though I usually preferred afternoon meetings, as I could keep focused and get more done in the mornings.

I typically took a lunch break when I didn't have a lunch meeting, which I scheduled once or twice a week. I always thought it was important to take thirty minutes to an hour for lunch in order to step away from work, relax, and enjoy the day.

After lunch, I dove right back into work. I spent the afternoon on the phone, sending emails, and getting work done for my clients. I always had several meetings each week, though I recommend not scheduling too many, as you need to spend time working on actual client work, studying, researching, and preparing for your next meetings.

Since the early days, my schedule has changed. I'm up by 6:30 am and by 7am I'm at the gym. I come back, shower, have breakfast with my family, play with my daughter and head to the office by 9 am I spend the first hour or so of each day doing high-level work without any distractions. Typically, on days I have calls, I start them at 10 am I used to work from home, but since the birth of my daughter, I find that having an outside office space gives me more quiet and more focus.

I work at the office from 10 am to about 4 pm, depending on the day. Sometimes I take off earlier, especially on Fridays. My schedule has become quite flexible, which is nice. After that, I go back home and spend the evening with my family. I might do a little bit of work at home later in the evening, if something is urgent, but most of the time, I'm done for the day.

Ultimately, my family is the most important thing, and that's why I do what I do. I get to make an impact and leave a legacy for my loved ones. More than that, I want to be present. My schedule now permits me to focus on that.

I start off my day with exercise to ensure that it gets done. As the day unfolds, and the work piles up, it becomes easier to push the exercise aside, so I make sure it happens first. Plus, I believe that exercise and health are critical components in success.

Consulting Success

My business is at the point where I can work from almost anywhere, so I travel with my family a lot more than I used to. We've spent time in Japan, Mexico, California, Malta, Europe, Toronto, and many other places. I'm able to get my work done in any of these places.

In the early days, it wasn't like that. I didn't have the same amount of freedom. Bear this in mind when you're starting out. Don't neglect your health or your family, but put in the hard work, stay focused, and you'll make progress faster. When you do, your schedule will eventually open up and provide you with a lot more flexibility.

Do you have to work twelve hours a day in the early stages of your business? No, definitely not. But if you want to reach success, you have to do the hard work and the long hours to get there. Later on, when you're traveling and enjoying more free time, you'll be glad you did.

How Much Money Can You Make as a Consultant?

So now you understand what's generally involved in becoming a consultant. We'll get into the details in upcoming sections of the book. What you're probably most interested in finding out is how much money you can make.

Is becoming a consultant a good source of income? The answer is a definite yes.

As I mentioned earlier, you can work hours that many people might consider part-time and still make $50,000 or more a year. Experienced consultants typically charge at least $200/hour. Some, myself included, charge over $10,000 a day and make at least $1 million a year.

You can hit these levels by doing several things to structure your business, pricing, and specialization. I'll cover all of them and more throughout this book, but don't expect to make this kind of money next week or next month.

If you put the principles I am going to teach you into practice and work on improving your business, you'll be well on your way to hitting new levels of success and making more money consistently.

Checklist: The Truth About Consulting

☐ I understand the challenges of becoming a consultant.

☐ I have identified the skills I am great at.

☐ I'm excited by the freedom and income potential of being a consultant, and I know I need to invest in my business in order to invest in myself.

☐ I will be successful, but it will take a lot of hard work; I must strive to keep learning.

CHAPTER 2:
SETTING UP YOUR CONSULTING BUSINESS

What Equipment Do You Need to Start Your Consulting Business?

Note: The information is this chapter will be most useful if you're just starting out or transitioning into the business. If you've already gotten past the basics of setting up your consulting business, I suggest you move on to the next chapter, where we get into more advanced concepts, techniques, and strategies.

Many trade publications and books claim you need a bunch of elaborate equipment to become a professional consultant, but getting started in this business is actually quite simple. You need an office. It can be a room in your house, your bedroom, whatever. It doesn't matter.

You need a telephone with voicemail. A dedicated line that is only for you and your business is important. Having voicemail is critical so that clients and prospective clients can leave you messages.

Tip: Most voicemail messages are boring. One way you can stand out is by making your voicemail more personable and interesting. Talk a bit about how you're "busy helping a client with _____ (insert whatever it is that you do)." If done properly, your voicemail will become part of your marketing materials. And in the game of being a consultant, the more ways you can stand out, the better.

It's helpful to have a fax number, but more people these days are simply scanning and emailing documents, so this isn't as necessary as it used to be.

You need a mailing address. These days, clients care less about where your office is located. If it's at your house in a residential area, that's fine. But you must have an address to give to clients, so they can send you documents and, most importantly, checks!

A computer and a fast internet connection go without saying.

That's it. That's all you need to get started, so let's move on to structuring your business.

Structuring Your Business

E very country is different, but I will address the biggest question I hear from people wanting to become consultants: "Should I incorporate?"

My general answer is no.

Disclaimer: This is not legal or financial advice, just my opinion from personal experience.

The only time you'll want to incorporate is if:

a) You're making substantial income. By "substantial," I mean if you're making quite a bit more money than you need to live on. When you're making more than you need, it's more tax effective to incorporate because your income will be taxed at a lower rate than if you're a personal business (often called a sole proprietor).

b) If you feel there's a good chance your business could get sued by your clients. Generally, this isn't a big issue for consultants because you can easily limit the number of people you work with. However, let's say you're an IT consultant, and you're making big changes to a client's IT infrastructure. If something goes wrong and the client sues you, you'll be in much better shape if you're incorporated.

Incorporation provides protection against personal liability.

If you're incorporated and get sued, only your business and the assets it has can be attacked. Your personal assets, such as your home and investments, are safe. If you're not incorporated and someone sues you and wins, all of your personal assets could be scooped up.

On the other hand, incorporating costs more money than registering as a personal business. Your accounting costs will also be substantially higher. So, it all comes down to what your needs are and what kind of consulting business you'll run.

It's best to meet with an accountant and go over your specific situation to find the right solution.

Using an Accountant

If you're not using an accountant for your consulting business, you're making a big mistake. When I started in this business, I thought I could do my own taxes. I was wrong. Working with an accountant is worth whatever they charge. Not only do accountants find ways to lower your taxes, but they'll help you deal with all the worries and issues regarding your money and taxes.

Accountants also tend to know many lawyers, so if you ever need to incorporate or deal with legal problems, they can definitely help.

Keeping Your Money Safe

I t's worthwhile to set up a bank account specifically for your consulting business. This gives you the ability to write checks with your company name on it, and more importantly, to receive payments written to your company name.

This looks more professional than having everything in your own name. It also gives the appearance that your company is bigger than it really is.

Having a business bank account also helps with tracking your finances. Setting up this kind of account shouldn't cost much, if anything, so it's a worthwhile step to take.

The Skinny on an Office

D o you really need an office? Many people believe that to be seen as a professional consultant you need your own office separate from your home.

While this used to be the case, these days, it just isn't true.

Not only will you save money by working from home, but it's more convenient and saves you the commuting time.

Most clients won't come to your office. Instead, you'll visit theirs. That being the case, it makes almost no sense for you to spend the money on a separate office if no one is going to visit it.

Having said that, there are some significant exceptions. I worked from home for years, but eventually, I began renting an office space. The change happened after the birth of my daughter. Suddenly, it became necessary to have a quiet space in which to work. If your home is filled with noise and activity throughout the day, you might consider an outside office, so you can concentrate and feel productive.

Some people simply can't concentrate when they're working from home. If you get distracted easily, or you want a very clear separation between work and home, getting a separate office might be of great benefit to you.

These days, many consultants prefer to use coworking spaces. A co-working space is an open office area that is shared by multiple independent professionals. For people who might otherwise work in isolation, these places offer a sense of communal gathering. They also tend to be quite affordable, and you can use the space as often as you want. Many coworking spaces provide conference rooms that you can schedule for client meetings.

Some of them also provide services such as fax machines, a mailing address, phones, even a secretary. If you're considering various outside options, this is something you should definitely look into.

Bear in mind, as an independent consultant, you have the freedom to work just about anywhere, as long as your location has internet and phone service. If you want to work on a tropical island, on a mountain top, in a cabin in the woods, you can do so, as long as you're able to connect your phone and laptop.

Figure out what works best for you and for your business. Once you've chosen a place to work, it's time to figure out how to stand out in the market. We'll look into that next.

Checklist: Setting up Your Consulting Business

☐ I have (or will soon acquire) the necessary equipment.

☐ I have structured my business as a personal business or an incorporation.

☐ I have spoken with an accountant to review which options are best

☐ I have a separate bank account for my business.

☐ I have chosen the best location in which to work.

CHAPTER 3:
THE AUTHORITY OF A SPECIALIST

Start as a Specialist, Not a Generalist

A sk yourself what it is that you do significantly better than most people. What is your area of expertise? What do people ask your advice and opinion about? Whatever that is, that's the area of consulting you should be in.

By now, you've likely decided what kind of consultant you want to be, so we won't spend much time on that. All I will say is be sure you have a passion for the area of consulting you choose.

More important, though, is the issue of specialization. When people ask what I do, I can say, "I'm a Marketing Consultant." That is accurate. But how many people do you know in marketing? Quite a few, I'd guess.

The problem with taking a general approach is that you get lost in the mix. There's nothing to make you stand out. That makes hiring you a more difficult decision for potential clients.

A better approach is to specialize. For example, I specialize in working with consultants to help them develop marketing systems that consistently attract their ideal clients, increase their fees, and win more proposals.

A Myth About Focus

Many consultants fear positioning themselves as specialists and focusing on a specific area of expertise. They think it will turn away a great deal of business. Maybe you have the same concern.

What I can tell you is, without a doubt, specializing and focusing your services is the way to go. Clients want to hire someone when they have a specific need, and if you can position yourself to fill that need with your specialization, you're more likely to get the job.

Choose one area that you can specialize in and make that the focus of your efforts. Your website and marketing materials, even your elevator pitch (I'll talk more on this later), should communicate your specialty.

As soon as you start focusing, you will see potential clients open up; they will be much more interested in your area of expertise than they would be in general skills.

Think of a wedding photographer. Many wedding photographers earn an amazing income. They charge $5,000 or more for a couple days of work.

That same photographer, if they market themselves as a general photographer who also does weddings, will not get nearly as much work. Nobody wants a generalist when they have a specific need in mind.

Two common ways to specialize are in systems and processes you've created or in a specific industry.

You can choose to package and hop, which is where you package the system and processes you've created and that have worked so effectively in one industry, and then you take them into another industry.

Let's say you work with car dealerships. You would take the system you've created with your car dealer clients and move it to, for example, the restaurant industry, applying it there.

The common myth is that "it might work for one industry, but it won't work in another!"

Nothing could be further from the truth. Most industries only apply the strategies and principles that everyone else in their industry applies. When you bring in a different set of strategies, they often provide significant results because they stand out so much from what everyone else in the industry is doing.

I was making a presentation once at the headquarters of a large pharmaceutical company. The President introduced me and told everyone why he had brought me in to help the company.

Consulting Success

I was about to start my presentation when one of managers said, "Hey, do you have any experience in our industry?"

At that time, I didn't. I'd worked with companies in over twenty-one industries, but not pharmaceuticals.

I locked eyes with the manager and replied, "No, I don't. But that's exactly why you need me. I bring a fresh perspective, and that's why Joe (the president) asked me to be here with you today."

Clearly, the status quo wasn't working for this company. Otherwise, they would not have brought me in.

Always be on the lookout for successful campaigns in other industries that you can bring to your clients. Most often, because no one else is doing it outside of that specific industry, bringing it into another industry could produce spectacular results.

Another option is to put all of your energy into one industry. If you help dentists with their marketing and patient communications, you may choose to become known as the "dentist marketing guru." This focus allows you to hone your skills in a specific area, so you can develop a name for yourself in that one industry.

That doesn't mean you should do what everyone else in that industry is already doing. Rather, you should develop a system of best practices from many industries and use them with your clients in their industry to help them achieve significant results.

At the same time, just because you focus your services on one area of specialty doesn't mean you can't help clients with other areas as they come up.

While I routinely help my clients with lead generation projects, they often ask for assistance with website copy and design, brochures and other marketing materials that my team can assist with.

There's nothing unique about my situation. This is generally how it works, and the reason is quite simple. Once a client sees that you can help them, they will want to pass you more and more work because they feel comfortable with you and trust you. So, pick your focus, communicate it, and watch the magic begin.

Getting your specialization wrong will cost you a lot of time and money.

It pays to get it right—the first time.

After working through our Specialization Worksheet, you'll be able to nail down your positioning with precision and confidence.

Access the worksheet and "level-up" from generalist to an in-demand specialist at consultingsuccess.com/bookbonus

---

The Most Lucrative Areas of Consulting

As I'm sure you're well aware, there are all kinds of consultants out there. You can make a very good living in almost any area of consulting.

Becoming a certain kind of consultant because you think it has bigger income potential is a bad move. You'll most likely find that you're unhappy because you aren't as passionate about the work. Becoming a successful consultant requires a lot of ongoing education and training, so you don't want to get stuck studying and learning about something that bores you.

That said, there are some points you need to consider in order to find the most lucrative opportunities.

1. Can You Demonstrate Results?

If the product that you deliver isn't visible and can't be measured in one form or another, you're not in a lucrative business.

Clients want to see results. They need to justify paying you, so if they can't see improvements, they have no reason to cough up the cash. Be sure that whatever you're doing for your clients, you have established a clear goal that is meaningful to both you and the client's business.

It could be increased sales, more leads, decreased costs, improved satisfaction rates, improved manufacturing speed—you get the point.

Make sure the work you do can be linked to results. By far, this is the most important weapon in a consultant's arsenal.

When push comes to shove, the consultant who can show they've delivered results will always land new projects and keep existing ones longer than someone who can't.

You don't need to be a magician. It's not necessary to move mountains with your results, and your clients aren't expecting you to do so.

Tip: Establish clear and consistent goals with your clients. Make sure they see value in the goal you've agreed upon. Also, make it something that you're confident you can accomplish. Promising something you can't deliver is a quick way to earn a bad reputation and end your work with that client. There's nothing wrong with gradual improvements, as long as that's what you and your client have agreed to.

2. Keep the Work Going

Now that you're showing your clients results, they have the incentive to continue paying you and giving you more work.

But if you structure your work so it's a one-time project, you've made a big mistake. It's not the end of the world, but you have to correct the situation.

To make the consulting business lucrative, you need to ensure that you've shown your clients a clear path for how you will continually help them improve their business and get results. By doing this, your clients become much more valuable to you. Instead of being worth a $3,000 project to you, they are worth $36,000 to you as you work with them over the year.

Your plan should show your overall process, and how when you do A for the client successfully, you can then work on B and then C.

Don't worry about sticking to this plan rigidly. Nothing goes in a straight line. Every client's business changes, their priorities change, but as long as you're doing good work, they will continually call on you for help.

3. Your Place in the Market

A lucrative consulting business needs a hungry market. Even if you generate the best results, if there aren't many people that want what you offer, you won't have much to go on.

These days, everyone is talking about niche businesses. Maybe you'll fill a gap in such an area. Regardless of whether the market is considered by others to be big or small, you must ensure that there is sufficient business to make it lucrative for you.

The other issue you need to consider is the severity of the need you will be filling. The more difficult a client perceives your work to be, in general, the more they will be willing to pay, making the project more lucrative.

Take a good look around and see what kind of need exists for the services you offer. Generally, if there are many other consultants in that area, or businesses that offer the kinds of services you do, it means that the market has a lot of opportunity—competition is a good thing.

Even in a crowded marketplace, a skillful consultant will find a way to stand out and become a sought-after advisor.

Standing Out in the Marketplace

You may be familiar with the 80/20 Rule. It's actually called Pareto's Principle. In this case, the principle states that 20 percent of the consultants in any given market will generate 80 percent of the business.

That means the other 80 percent are fighting over the remaining 20 percent.

This principle holds true. Look at real estate agents. The top 20 percent have sales and incomes far higher than others in their market.

How can you become one of those consultants in the top 20 percent? First, you need to stand out. If no one can find you, you're not going to get significant business.

Standing out takes many forms:

1. Market Yourself so People Can Find You

You can get out and network, put targeted ads online and in trade publications, write articles and much more. Marketing your services is a critical aspect of every consultant's business.

One powerful way to get your name out there and establish expertise is by answering people's questions—and doing it for free!

As part of your total marketing strategy, answering people's questions is well worth your time. Social media provides effective ways for you to get out there and communicate your expertise.

Have you ever heard of Gary Vaynerchuk? You know, the Crush It man? Gary is a marketing thought leader, and he built his Wine Library TV website (which, in turn, helped sell millions of dollars of wine at his family's store) by making a name for himself answering people's questions.

Gary hit the wine forums and every relevant website he could find. He answered people's questions and commented in detailed and thoughtful ways.

Guess what happened? People started noticing him. They saw that he knew what he was talking about, and they wanted to know more.

He established his credibility, became an authority, and made a name for himself. You can make this work for your business, too.

For example, jump in to a LinkedIn or Facebook group and engage with other professionals. Start making a name for yourself.

Don't just intrude into conversations in order to promote your services, however. The more value you provide, the more you'll get noticed. Add your name, company name, and website address at the bottom of each reply, so people can start to recognize you.

You can do this on forums, LinkedIn, blogs, and other websites. It's good for marketing, branding, credibility building, and it offers SEO benefits.

2. Make an Impact

Have you ever noticed how the people with the wildest personalities, the ones who do things that people talk about in the news, are the ones who stand out the most?

I'm not suggesting that you go out and perform a stunt to get people's attention, though that is an idea.

What you need to do is find a way to make yourself different from all the other consultants in your industry.

There are several ways to do this:

Your branding. Your name, design, and image can make you stand out in the marketplace. Many companies have successfully used branding to their advantage. You can do the same.

Your price. You can charge much less than your competition, though I don't recommend this. Or you charge much more, as long as you're providing more value and people are willing to pay for it.

Your guarantee. It takes confidence in your services to offer clients a guarantee. For instance, I offer my clients a guarantee that they will see the results we've agreed on, and if they aren't happy, I will continue to work with them at no cost until those results are achieved. Not many people are willing to do this. If you are, you'll instantly pique the interest of prospective clients.

Professional communications. Be professional. It's amazing how many consultants call themselves professional yet fail to return their clients calls on time or follow through as promised. If you take action right away, communicate and act like a real professional, people will take notice. This builds a level of trust with your clients. When you're dependable and deliver results, your clients will have little reason to give their business to anyone else.

3. Make It Easy to Contact You

When a potential client needs your services, they're going to try to contact you either by email or by phone. If you don't answer or reply right away, or if you make it hard for them to get in touch with you, you can kiss their business goodbye.

Business owners don't have the time or patience to try repeatedly to contact a consultant. If you don't make it easy, they'll find someone else.

4. Be Excellent

Marketing your services, making an impact, and being available are all great ways to all stand out, but they are parts of something bigger, something that can position you well above your competitors: Excellence.

The service at most restaurants is average, so when you walk into a place and get blown away by the extra care and attention, when the décor looks amazing, the food is great, and the staff is super friendly, you notice. Excellence makes an impression. You can't ignore it.

Being average, even being good, might get you a mention from time to time, but when you're excellent at what you do, people can't stop talking about you.

Consulting Success

So, how excellent are you at what you do?

Being excellent isn't about being the best—it's about being better than most of the others around you. Most people know they could be doing better. They could sharpen their skills, learn new strategies, invest their own money into new products and testing, yet most people fail to do this.

Part of learning new strategies is being open to learning from industries other than your own. Too many businesses stay so focused on their industry that they fail to see the ocean of opportunities surrounding them each and every day.

Can a marketing strategy used by realtors help your consulting business? Absolutely. What about a furniture company's direct mail that you keep receiving? Or that loyalty program you just signed up for at your local bookstore? Do you think you could learn from of these and apply them in your business?

Are the books and magazines you're reading only about your own industry? If you're in marketing, do you only read marketing books? Broaden your scope. Start reading about psychology, about selling and productivity, and you'll quickly discover new ideas and concepts that you can benefit and make money from.

This lesson should be applied to your consulting clients, as well. Always be on the lookout for successful campaigns in other industries that you can bring to your clients.

Excellence requires taking action. When I say "taking action," I don't mean writing an article, fixing your website, making an advertisement, writing a consulting proposal. All of those are important, but they are what I call "building."

By taking action, I mean picking up the phone and setting up meetings with prospective customers. Getting out of your office and meeting with potential buyers. Spending money on actual marketing and advertising.

Consultants and business owners will do anything they can to delay doing these things, even though they know that they need to do them. Many people find them uncomfortable. They don't like calling people out of the blue. Or requesting meetings. Or spending their money. But that's what separates the successful people from the ones who only talk about success.

Want to be excellent? Take out a piece of paper right now and write down all the things you KNOW you should do for your business that you keep delaying for one reason or another.

Once you've got that list, each day or a couple times a week, DO one of them. Don't think about it—just do it! The results will astound you.

Expand your horizons. When you're excellent, you go beyond where most others dare to venture.

Take a good look at your business and yourself. Be honest. Think about the care you give to your clients, the results that you deliver, and the skills you have compared to others in your market. Are you just average, good, or excellent at what you do?

Excellence doesn't happen overnight. But commit to achieving it, and you'll get there soon. And when you do, all your hard work will pay off.

Checklist: Becoming a Specialist

- ☐ I'm going to specialize in the consulting area of _____.

- ☐ I can demonstrate that I achieve results for my clients.

- ☐ There is a market for my services.

- ☐ I will structure my consulting projects to provide ongoing work.

- ☐ I have a plan for how I will stand out in the marketplace.

- ☐ It's easy for potential clients to contact me.

- ☐ I understand what it takes to be excellent and have a plan to make it happen.

CHAPTER 4:
BRANDING AND
YOUR CONSULTING BUSINESS

What's Really in a Name?

Deciding what to call your consulting business is always a challenge. Some people decide it's easiest to use their actual name, like Thomson Consulting. The problem with this choice is that it can sound boring.

However, as long as your name is easy to spell and pronounce, your business name will be too. If you're structuring your business where *you* are the brand, where a buyer is going to reach out to you because they see you as the expert, then using your name as the business name makes sense.

If your plans and goals are to create a business that is much larger than you, where there are going to be many other consultants or staff as part of the business, it makes sense to consider a name that conveys much more about what you do as a consulting firm. If you're planning to grow and sell the business down the road, having the name directly attached to your personal name doesn't make sense.

Others use acronyms, but these often lack meaning, and no one knows what to call them. They often get lost in the midst of all the other acronym names out there. Do you really want to be another ABC Consulting or XYZ Marketing?

Another option is to create a descriptive name, something that reveals the nature of your business. If you go that way, make sure the name isn't boring.

Some companies simply invent words to use as the company name, such as Snapple or Google. The strength of these names is their uniqueness, though they don't actually communicate any specific message.

The most popular route is to use an experiential name, like Explorer or Navigator. These make sense to consumers, as they communicate a specific experience. Just make sure yours stands out.

A final option is to create an evocative name. These are sometimes a bit unusual, but that is intentional. They have an underlying positioning that is meant to garner attention. Examples include Yahoo, Apple, and Virgin.

You never get a second chance to make a good first impression, and that is true in business names as well. You want to make sure that potential customers can easily look you up, so deliberate misspelling or strange punctuation with the name (delicio.us, for example) can throw people off.

This is especially true when you are just getting started and people are largely unfamiliar with your services. Consider how customers will pronounce the name. Will it sound confusing? Does it set you apart from all of the other consultants in your field?

Whichever way you choose to go, remember that an effective name is attached to a brand. Most people don't buy from a company called ABC or from a company called Tesla or Heinz or General Electric because they think it's a cool name. They make a buying decision based on the brand behind the name.

Using Design to Your Advantage

Some consultants are led to believe that they need an elaborately designed website and marketing materials. They are often pushed to this conclusion by designers who have little to no experience in the business of consulting.

As someone who previously owned a branding and design firm for several years and now runs a consulting business, allow me to dispel the myths and dish you out a plate of truth.

Design is extremely powerful. It can help create a strong first impression, which is critical.

But design, in and of itself, will not win you business. A beautifully designed brochure goes into the recycling bin unless it has persuasive copy and proof that grabs the attention of the reader.

On many occasions, I have won projects valued at over $100,000 without a fancy brochure or expensive business cards.

Consulting Success

Designers are chosen based on their design skills. You'd be a fool to work with a designer who has an unprofessional looking website or portfolio.

Consultants on the other hand are selected based on their results.

Simple Marketing Materials

L et me give you an example of the marketing materials I have used successfully for many years.

1. Website

A simple website that speaks directly to my target customer. I avoid "we" in favor of "you," speaking directly to clients. My website clearly breaks down the services I offer and how my clients and prospective clients will benefit from them. I list who my clients are, which is a great credibility factor, and I provide pages of testimonials from satisfied clients. That's it. No moving graphics. No flashy pictures. It's simple, to the point, and looks professional.

Will my website win a creative award? No chance. But does it win business? You bet!

2. Business Card

A business card is one of your best tools to make a first impression. That said, you don't need to spend a lot of money for fancy colors and graphics. I've used a black-and-white, double-sided business card for years.

It works. It lays out all of my contact information clearly and has a very direct message that tells my target market what I can do for them. Again, very simple, cheap to print, and works like a charm.

3. Brochure

I don't have a formal brochure. I've never bothered to make one. Instead, I have a two-page printout that I create on my black and white laser printer. It explains what my business does, how I help companies, and it's filled with testimonials. It also provides my contact information.

This is a much smarter approach, in my opinion, than paying for the printing of an expensive brochure, since it allows you to update information at any time and make adjustments as necessary for each client meeting.

That's it. The point is, when you're starting out, you shouldn't worry about creating fancy marketing materials.

If your target customers are Fortune 500 companies, you may need to create more formal materials, but I've worked with billion-dollar companies who didn't require such materials in order to win their business.

When it comes down to it, clients only care about results. Your reputation is molded around the results that you provide. Soon enough, you'll be generating a significant amount of your business through referrals. When that happens, you surely won't need any fancy materials to pick up new clients.

Keeping It Lean

It's best to run your consulting business as lean as possible. Don't spend money when you don't have to, and definitely don't spend it on things that don't help you build your business.

I'm not suggesting that professional design is a waste of money. On the contrary, it can be a powerful differentiator. What I want to make clear is that it's usually unnecessary to spend hundreds or thousands of dollars on fancy materials when you're just starting out.

It's smarter to create functional materials early on, and later, when you have more money coming in, then you can look at spending more to update your professional image.

Design Resources to Save You Time and Money

Now that you understand what design can and can't do for you, let us share some great online design resources that make the design process as simple and cheap as possible.

For example, several websites allow you to submit a brief of what you are looking for, whether a logo, business card design, website, or something else. You set your budget, and within a day or two, you start seeing designs custom-made for you by many designers. It's not uncommon to receive fifty design options. The beauty of this service is that you only choose the designs you like, and you can request revisions. You only pay for the one you want to use.

A few services you might want to look into include: 99Designs, CrowdSpring, and Ink'd.

There's no better way to get professional design at a low cost and with rapid turnaround times than with services like these.

When it comes to creating a website that will attract clients, the key is to design for the user. Make the information you present highly readable by using bullet points, lists, bolded texts, and other visual cues. Always include pictures of yourself and your team, so clients know that you're a real person. That generates trust. Contact information is essential, of course.

Think carefully about the impact of the colors you use on your website. According to Derek Halpern of Social Triggers, the biggest mistake website owners make is to mix passive and action colors. Passive colors are the colors that make up your brand identity and image, while action colors tell people that they can take an action.

For example, if your logo color is blue, that's a passive color for your website. Don't use it on a button or link. Instead, use an action color like red or orange. This might sound pedantic, but it actually helps guide potential clients to your services.

Try to create relationships with potential clients through your website by offering further information. For example, allow them to enter their email address in order to receive a free valuable report or newsletter.

Ultimately, the most important aspect of your website is to communicate the value of your services to prospective clients. Your value proposition needs to clearly and concisely articulate what you do, who you do it for, and why you are a better choice than the competition. Your landing page, in particular, needs to provide essential information about you, your services, and your reputation.

It's helpful to include testimonials from satisfied clients. They add to your credibility, but make sure they are specific. Don't include testimonials that only provide vague compliments.

Finally, make sure you have an analytics service installed to track your website's statistics. Google Analytics and StatCounter are two great, free options. The data you gather from these services will guide you on how to improve your website.

Are you losing clients due to your unimpressive consulting website? Four out of five buyers look at your website before doing business with you.

We've created a guide on the 5 Elements of An Effective Consulting Website to make sure your website is helping you instead of hurting you.

Learn how to turn your website into a powerful tool to position you as a trusted advisor at consultingsuccess.com/bookbonus

---

Checklist: Branding and Your Business

☐ My consulting business name is meaningful, easy to remember, and impactful.

☐ I have a business card that is simple yet impactful.

☐ I've created a functional brochure that clearly outlines my services.

☐ My website includes the key information a prospective client would want to see and read.

CHAPTER 5:
STRATEGIES FOR CONSULTING FEES AND PRICING

Which Pricing Structure Should You Use?

There are several ways you can determine how to set your consulting rates and fees.

There is no right or wrong way to go about this, as long as you get paid what is sustainable to grow your business.

The worst thing you can do as a consultant is undercharge. The exception is if you've just become a consultant and want to get your feet wet. In that case, taking on some lower-paying work to establish yourself, build a client list, and test your skills is a smart move.

However, in most cases, you don't want to undercharge as clients will undervalue your services. In general, the more you charge, the greater the perception clients will have of the value of your services.

Before you jack up your fees to the moon, make sure they're set in a logical way.

The Consultant's Status Quo

First, figure out what prices other consultants are charging and set fees accordingly.

By doing this, you instantly position yourself with established consultants. This is good standard to begin with, but be careful lumping yourself in with everyone else.

Look at the most successful people around you. They tend to speak their minds and have their own unique characteristics. Put simply, they are different than others around them.

In consulting, you're after the same thing. Position yourself as different from the competition. Being different is not enough by itself, however. You also need to deliver results and value.

A Simple Formula to Help You Set Your Fees

Figure out what you want to make per year.

If your goal is $80,000, take that number and divide it by the number of hours you have available to work each year.

Start with fifty-two weeks, subtract vacation time, holidays, and sick days. What you're left with is usually about forty-five weeks. Assuming you spend about forty hours a week working, then you can figure out your total hours worked per year through simple multiplication:

So, 45 weeks x 40 hours of work = 1,800

New consultants often take this number and divide it by their goal salary. In this case, it would be 80,000/1800 = $44.44, which would be your hourly rate.

BUT there is a huge issue being overlooked here. You won't actually be working with clients for 1,800 hours a year.

Why? Because you need to spend some of that time on marketing, administration, and the general duties required to run and grow your consulting business.

You'll probably end up spending 50 percent of your time on actual client work, so divide your 1,800 hours by two. Your new total is 900 hours of billable work.

Now, divide your goal salary of $80,000 by the 900 hours of billable work:

80,000/900 = $88.88 an hour

What this tells you is how much you need to work and at what fee in order to hit your goal of an $80,000 salary.

If your goal is lower, your fee will be lower. If you want to spend less time but make the same amount of money, you'll need to raise your fee. This is a sliding scale and provides you with an idea of how to set your rates.

Let's not stop there, because we can and should take this another step.

The above rate of $88.88 is fine as a base rate, but we haven't taken into account all the overhead and other costs associated with running a business.

If your annual overhead is $10,000 (rent, phone, internet, supplies, insurance, medical, etc.) take this number and divide it by the number of billable hours. In the above example, it would be $10,000/900 = $11.11

So, your previous rate of $88.88 would now be 88.88 + 11.11 = $99.99. Round that off, and your "real" hourly rate is $100.

While I usually discourage charging clients an hourly rate (more about that later), having an understanding of what to charge per hour is helpful.

That's because many fee structures, like a project fee, daily, or half-day fee, all require you to know what your hourly fee is.

Let's get into some other fee structures that you should consider.

Project Fee

You can move away from hourly work and into a project-based fee structure. In this case, you need to determine how many hours you expect the project to take.

I recommend adding an additional 50 percent to the expected hours you think it will take to complete the project. This allows for administration and overflow. Put simply, things always take longer than you initially expect them to, and you don't want to end up losing money on the project. This padding gives you protection, which is why it's a common practice in the industry. Adjust this additional percentage as needed.

The fact is, even with project fees, you still need to know what your hourly fee is so that you can estimate what it will take to complete the project.

Daily Consulting Fee

Some consultants prefer to bill by the day or half-day. There's nothing wrong with this approach, but you still need to know what your hourly rate is so you can calculate your daily fee.

For example, if your hourly fee is $200/hour and you'll be spending eight hours at your client's office, you might charge $1,600 for the day.

But there are a few other things for you to consider.

Travel Time

How long will it take you to reach your client's location? If it's only a few minutes, no big deal. But if you need to spend one hour each way to get there and back, that's two hours out of your day that you could otherwise be billing for.

In that case, your eight-hour day has become a 10-hour day, and there's nothing wrong with charging an extra $400 for the day to compensate. Do you have to charge this? Of course not. That's completely up to you. But it's definitely worth considering.

Travel Expenses

If a company asks you to make a presentation at a location outside of your city or state, they should pay for your travel costs. When a Japanese client asked me to moderate a panel presentation, the company paid for my airfare, accommodation, and daily fee.

Prefer to travel business or first class? That depends on your relationship with the client and how much of a name you've made for yourself. If you're well established in the industry and in high demand, it's standard practice to ask for and expect business class travel.

On the other hand, if you're just getting started building your name in the market, you shouldn't expect business class travel. In fact, I'd recommend against asking for it.

Meals and More

Consultants often ask us if they should include the cost of food and drinks in their daily rate. I've never done this. It seems unprofessional to take it to that level.

You have to eat regardless of whether you're at your client's location or at home, so unless the city you're in only has $150 meals, you should swallow the cost of meals and drinks on the job.

When you're on the job, you won't have much time for leisurely lunches anyway. In fact, most of the time you'll only have ten to twenty minutes to grab a quick bite before you go back to work. Often, your client will provide lunch for you on-site or take you out for lunch.

Justifying Your Fees Through Value

N ow you have an idea of what kind of hourly fee you need to charge in order to earn the annual income you desire, and that means you also know what you need to charge on a daily, weekly, and monthly basis to achieve it.

However, charging on an hourly or daily basis only allows so much room for growth. If you want to make $300,000 a year, it's hard to ask a prospective client to pay you $1,000 an hour. Maybe you're worth it, but most companies will be scared away by a number like that. Is there a way to generate a higher income for yourself without scaring away prospective clients? Yes, there is.

How about when a prospective or current client says your fees seem too high? Is there an effective way to deal with this? Yes, there is.

The answer to both of these situations comes from creating value for your clients and then justifying your fees based not on hours, but on the value your client will receive from your services.

When I speak of value, I'm not referring to touchy-feely customer service or the high-quality mumbo jumbo that so many people throw around. I am talking about tangible value.

Making Value Count

Experienced consultants often charge 10 times more than new consultants. This is partly due to the fact that they have more experience, but it's also because they know how to justify value to their clients.

Explain to your clients what they will get out of your services. For example, your client might want you to solve a problem that has been causing a lot of trouble. If your solution is valuable, you can and should be setting your rate using value and ROI-based consulting fees.

This begins by asking the right questions. Let me give you an example that can be applied to every kind of consulting.

Let's say I'm referred to an insurance business that wants help increasing their sales. I meet with the president of the company, and after listening to him describe the current situation, I see how I can help. I tell the president my fees are $10,000 a month and that I usually start off with an agreement to work together for four months, but he can cancel at any time if his company is not satisfied. Hearing my fee, the president does a double take.

"$10,000 a month," he thinks. "That's a lot!"

To justify the value of my fee I might ask him how much each client on average is worth to him? I would then ask how many new clients the company brings in each month? I may also ask how much they currently spend to bring in those new clients?

By the way, you should get all of this information before discussing your fee with clients.

With that information, I can craft a case for the value I will deliver. Let's say the company currently estimates that each new client is worth $10,000, that they currently bring in 10 new clients a month, and that it costs $25,000 to bring in those new clients each month.

I now know that the company is bringing in roughly $100,000 in new business each month. However, they spend $25,000 bringing in that new business, so they net about $75,000 monthly on new business. They also have many other fees for their office, employees, and so on, but you get the idea.

Knowing what I now know, I tell the president of the company that I believe I can lower their marketing and advertising costs by 50 percent (to $12,500 per month) through testing and tracking, and they'll still see the same results in terms of new business.

I also believe that improving their current ads and lead handling system will bring in an additional two clients each month (worth an additional $20,000 each month).

I could keep going and show the company how I could save them more money or make them more by using different strategies through the knowledge and experience I have.

The result is that I have shown the president how his company can make an additional $32,500 each month with my help. I clarify that this won't happen right away, but suggest that perhaps we agree that within four months of working together, these will be the results.

Now, if I'm making this company an extra $25,000 each month, or $300,000 a year (gains minus my fee) don't you think they would be more than happy to pay?

This is how you justify your fees with value. You don't have to be increasing sales; you can be reducing expenses, speeding up a process that will result in improved revenue.

Just remember, business owners think in terms of money. Whatever you use to show the value you will create, always tie it back to what that means for them in dollars and cents.

The Pricing Structure Consultants Love

One of the biggest challenges you'll face as a consultant, especially in the early days, is creating a stable income.

By stable income, I don't mean getting a paycheck every two weeks like a typical employee. I'm referring to a continuous flow of client work.

When you do hourly or project work, you schedule often looks like this: You go to work, tackle whatever client issue you're working on, and you're done. You send the invoice, get paid, and don't hear from that client again until they need more work. Sounds good, right? Sure, it's standard practice.

The big problem with this is that you need an ever-increasing pool of clients so that when one project is over, you can go right into the next one. Some clients only have a one-time project, or they drop off for whatever reason, so you need to be continuously adding to your client base.

Why a Consulting Retainer Makes This Better:

When you set up a retainer agreement with your client, essentially you work with them for certain number of hours each month and bill them monthly.

Here's what you need to do to make it work:

1) Have a plan for what will be accomplished each month, or a clearly defined set of deliverables that both you and the client have agreed upon.

2) Each week or, at minimum, each time you meet with the client, show them what has been achieved or completed prior to the meeting. That way they can see the progress and feel the momentum.

3) Always plan ahead. At each meeting, don't simply review what you've completed. Also, discuss what you plan to accomplish next. How formal you make these plans should depend on the client. I've had some clients who require a status of the project every two weeks to one month with figures and data. Others just want to talk about it.

4) Deliver. This one's critical. I know it sounds obvious, but the whole reason consulting retainers work is because you make things happen and your client is willing to pay you on an ongoing basis to continue the work.

The next time you're showing a client your fees or sending a proposal or bid for a project, be sure to build in an option for monthly retainer work.

The consulting retainer setup works better for both you and your client. You get the stability of having a few clients who provide steady work and income.

Also, because you don't have to chase down as many new clients, you can focus better on your existing clients' business, give them more of your time, and deliver better results. The consulting retainer works. I've used it for many years, and it can be a great way to work.

Win More Projects with Pricing Plans

Clients love having options. One of the most effective pricing strategies is the strategy of three.

Here's how it works:

Offer your clients three packages. You can call them bronze, silver, and gold, or anything else that makes sense for your business. The names aren't important; it's the concept and the psychology behind them that makes the strategy work.

Your first offering is your bronze package. This is your least expensive plan and includes the fewest number of hours spent with your client or fewest deliverables.

The silver plan is more expensive and goes beyond the basic services of your bronze plan. This one offers more value, more of your time, or more deliverables.

The gold plan is the most expensive. This is your all-in, total-support, complete high-roller package. The cost isn't the only thing that increases with this plan; you'll deliver far more value to your client. Your time with them might increase, you might use better systems or a wider advertising reach, or maybe you'll manage and implement more aspects of the strategy you've set.

The key is that your price increases as you deliver more value to your clients. Remember, this shouldn't just be a bunch of frills and gimmicks, but actual services that your clients will find more valuable for their business.

Seventy to 80 percent of the time, you'll find clients take the middle (silver) package. This is where the psychology kicks in. Most clients don't want the cheapest, and they find it hard initially to justify the most expensive, so they take the middle ground.

As a consultant, this works out great for you. When you only offer one option to your clients, then the only decision they have to make is whether or not to hire you. That is the equivalent of telling them it's your way or the highway. By providing options, you make the decision process easier and more satisfying for them.

Offering two packages also works, but I would never offer more than three. It gets too confusing, and the last thing you want to do is complicate your clients' purchasing decision.

How Consultants Can Get Very Rich

There's only so much time in each day and only one of you, so how do you go from making a good income to making an amazing income?

Partner with a client. Not in the legal sense of becoming joint owners in the business, but in regard to sharing the revenue or savings generated as a result of your work.

I've given this a go a couple of times, and it's not the easiest thing to do well. But when it works, it's by far the best way to make an incredible income.

There are other ways to leverage your skills to grow your business. The first is by creating a consulting tool that you can sell to clients. The second is by hiring others to help build your business. I'll touch on these later, but for now, let's explore the pitfalls and opportunities of partnering with a client to get rich.

Here's how it works. You agree with your client that you won't take any payments or fees for your work. In return, you receive a percentage of the revenues or savings that you produce for your client's business. This can be anywhere from 5 to 50 percent.

Why would your client turn over 50 percent of their money to you? Because it means they don't have to put up any money in advance, and they only have to pay you when they make more money. They may not make as much, but it's a sure thing, and they will be happy knowing they have someone on their side who can produce results.

In actual numbers, this means if you boost your client's business by $500,000 a year, $250,000 would be yours. Of course, you must have confidence that you can produce results. If you can't, you're wasting your time and that of your clients.

It sounds good, but it's not easy work. You have to completely trust the client. If you don't have a solid relationship with them, this arrangement is almost guaranteed to deliver you nothing but stress, frustration, and little to no money.

I recommend that consultants work at least one or two projects successfully to completion with the client first. If all goes well, you'll be in a much better position to entertain the idea of partnering and sharing in the profits.

This setup won't work for every kind of consulting business. If it can work for yours, it's definitely something worth exploring as you begin completing projects for clients.

Does A Lower Fee Mean More Clients?

If you've been asking yourself this question, you're not alone. It's very common. Some who are new to consulting believe that by lowering their fees they'll attract more business.

In their minds, lowering their price means lowering the barrier for clients to hire them.

They're wrong. Lowering your fees is a huge mistake.

When you charge less than everyone around you, you quickly become known as the cheapest provider of such services. Do people usually place a premium on things that cost more? Yes. Do they assume that something must be better quality if it costs more? Yes, again.

Regardless of how good you are at what you do, charging less positions you as offering less value to prospective clients.

So, not only will fewer companies be interested in your services, but you'll make less from each one, which means you'll need many more clients in order to reach the same income level as a competitor who charges more.

Why You Need to Charge More

One of the biggest mistakes new consultants make is undercharging for the services they provide. As mentioned earlier, if you're brand new to the business, there's nothing wrong with giving your first few clients a great deal to win their business, prove your skills, and get the referral engine running.

That said, even if you're new, you should make it very clear to those first few clients that you're offering a special deal, and that after the first project or month, you will need to charge your regular rates.

Now, back to the big mistake many consultants make—undercharging. Consultants usually do this for two reasons. First, they see others around them charging that price, or they read it somewhere online. And second, they believe that having a lower fee than others will give them a competitive advantage.

I've already explained why price can't be a competitive advantage for consultants, and the danger of lumping yourself in with all the others in your industry is just as dangerous, because you become just another average consultant.

The bigger problem, however, is that undercharging leads to consultants running around in circles. Because their fees are lower, they have to work more hours and have more clients to reach the income level they want. That doesn't make good business sense.

On the other hand, by having higher fees, you're able to focus your time, energy, and resources on fewer clients, work fewer hours, and make more money. That's the approach all consultants should take.

How to Increase Your Fees

Knowing that you should increase your fees, the question is how do you go about doing this, both with new clients and existing ones?

Increasing Fees for New Clients

This situation is the easy one to deal with. You might be charging $100 an hour and believe that you should increase your fees to $120 or $150 an hour to cover growing expenses, the cost of hiring a contractor or part-time employee, or simply because you feel you should be earning more. Whatever your reason, just start telling prospective clients your new rate when you meet with them. It's as simple as that.

Increasing Fees for Existed Clients

Increasing fees with existing clients is more challenging. I get a lot of questions about this from consultants, because they're afraid of doing it.

By far their biggest concerns are that they'll lose clients or face objections. Let's explore how to increase your fees the right way, so you're well equipped to handle it.

The first step to successfully increasing your fees is deciding what your new rate will be. To determine this, go back and read over the section on calculating your rates. Plug in your new target income and expenses, and you'll quickly figure out what your new rate should be. If you're switching from an hourly rate to a project rate or some other structure, that's fine. Follow the guide I outlined before, and write down how you plan to charge clients and what fee you'll ask for.

The second step is by far the most important. It's the secret ingredient, and one that, unfortunately, many consultants miss. The critical step we are talking about is deciding what additional value you will provide to your clients.

For example, if you're currently charging $2,000 a month for a full day at your client's factory, where you complete an intensive review and follow-up recommendations on how they can improve certain areas of their business, but you want to raise your fee to $2,500 a month, maybe you can also provide free weekly monitoring, phone support, or some other product or service your client will appreciate.

The reason you must provide real or perceived additional value to your clients when increasing your fees is because they find it much easier to justify paying more when they get more. Even if the additional value you provide doesn't actually cost you much, or take you much extra time, as long as your clients see an increase in value, they will be much more accepting of your new fee.

The next step is to communicate your price increase with your client. You can do this by sending them an email or letter, though I always prefer to do it in person or on the phone. Whatever form of communication you choose, always send something in written form, so your client can see the details with their own eyes. This prevents confusion later on about what was or wasn't said.

Once you have that conversation and send the letter to your client, it's extremely important to explain the additional value your clients will receive. You must do this in a way that makes sense to them.

For example, if you're going to provide maintenance of their website or advertising campaign, simply saying it is not enough. Tell your client about the additional benefits they'll receive from this new service.

Will they save time, money, increase their efficiency, their conversions, or something else? Whatever the benefits are, spell them out in crystal-clear language.

Your letter should also state why you're increasing fees. Saying that you're doing it because you want to make more money isn't a good move. Explain it properly. If your costs have gone up, you can mention that. I have always found telling clients that my fees will be increasing because I now have new technology, staff, or resources that will help them grow their business, to be an effective strategy.

Remember, it all comes down to value. Show your clients how they will get more value, explain why your fees will be increasing, and then communicate it clearly with your clients.

If more than several of your clients are dead set against the fee increase, it probably means you haven't included enough additional value to justify the increase in their minds, or maybe you didn't communicate the benefits clearly enough.

You might lose a client from time to time when you increase your fees. Don't worry, that's part of the business. Increasing your fees means you can make the same amount of money with fewer clients, and as you continue to market your business and pick up new clients at your higher rate, your consulting business will become even more profitable.

Equity Vs. Cash: Opportunity or Danger

Some consultants find themselves in a position where a prospective client offers equity or stock in their business instead of paying cash.

What this means is that the company is offering a certain number of shares or a percentage in their business.

When Working with a Public Company

If the company is publicly traded, meaning they are listed on a stock exchange, then your shares in that company actually have cash value. You can sell those shares, and they'll be worth whatever the market value is that day.

However, if the share price tanks, you might find that your $20,000 in shares quickly become worth $20—that's a danger.

On the other hand, if the company has great prospects (the next Google, maybe) your $20,000 in shares could be worth $200,000 or $2,000,000 depending on the company, market, and economy, among other factors.

Put simply, you're taking a chance. If you believe that the company has potential and you are okay with the risk of your shares becoming virtually worthless, taking stock in a publicly traded company is worth considering.

When Working with a Private Company

I f the business is a private company and offers you shares, what they are offering is actually nothing more than a piece of paper. There is a small chance the company will go public one day, or get bought out, and in those situations, your shares could have some value attached to them.

When you consider the high percentage of companies that go out of business within five years, taking shares instead of payment in a private company is risky business.

In my early years as a consultant, I made the mistake of taking a number of equity/share payment deals. In one situation, when I consulted for an energy company, I held 500,000 shares in their business. The prospects for them to go public looked good.

If the share price had reached $2, I would have had a million dollars. Unfortunately, that was a big IF. The company faced trouble a year later, and my shares are still worthless today.

Consulting Success

Most of the time, when I've accepted shares, I wound up with a nice piece of paper that looked impressive, had a lot of numbers on it, yet had no money attached to it.

I recommend that consultants stand their ground and demand cash. If the company won't offer cash, politely decline the opportunity and move on.

Then again, if you believe the company has strong growth potential, accepting payment in part-cash and part-stock option could be lucrative.

Private companies are a big gamble, however. Nine times out of ten, the stock will lose value.

Average Consulting Rates

It seems like every other day a consultant asks me, "What's the average rate a consultant should charge?" My reply is always the same, "There isn't one. It all depends."

You see, too many variables exist to have one single average rate. Your country, your industry, your level of experience, the level of results you generate for your clients, your positioning and area of specialization are some of the factors that determine your rate.

Don't worry about the average. It's always a good idea to know what others are charging, but that shouldn't influence your rates too much if you've followed my advice earlier in this book.

To find out what others are charging, you can attend an industry or networking event in your area and ask others there. You can search the Internet and call up a few consultants.

Pretend you're a potential client, or even better, just tell them you're getting started and wondering what is standard in the industry.

Pricing for International Clients

I f you are consulting with clients outside of your country, there are a few things to consider when it comes to setting your fee.

The first is to ensure that your international client knows your standard rates and is able to pay them. You don't want to spend time trying to win a client only to find out they can't afford your fees. This applies to both international and local clients.

Once you've determined that everything is good on that front, the next thing to consider is the rates for your type of work in your client's country. If they are far lower than what you normally charge, you'll have to decide whether it's worth your time and effort.

If their rates are generally higher, you may be able to get paid more than you usually charge. And if you provide a service that isn't readily available to your international client in their home country, you can often charge substantially more—again, as long as you're providing real value.

Consulting Success

When I've consulted for companies in Japan, I often charge fees that North American companies would never consider paying.

Why? Because to Japanese companies, I am a specialist. I provide a skill set and level of expertise that they couldn't find in their own market. They had the funds, faced a challenge that required a solution, and were willing to pay for it. I simply filled their need by providing the solution they were looking for.

Research the market, understand the local rate structure, and evaluate the need you're filling. Doing this will give you insight into how to charge your international clients.

Tips on What to Avoid

No matter the pricing structure you decide on, a few things can derail entire projects from the beginning. A big mistake many new consultants make is replying to toxic questions from clients too quickly. I call them toxic because if you answer them too quickly, they can be the death of your project, even before you get started.

Two of the most common questions that clients ask consultants are:

- How long will it take to complete?

- How much will it cost?

Simple questions. Innocent as they may seem, they are actually quite loaded.

I'm not saying your client is doing anything wrong. On the contrary, I'd ask the same questions if I was in their shoes.

But, that doesn't mean you should answer them right away.

While you might feel that failure to answer these questions right away shows a lack of confidence and knowledge, this couldn't be farther from the truth.

That may sound counterintuitive, but it is the case. For example, let's say you rush to answer your client's question. You blurt out, "It'll take three to four weeks, and I don't think it'll cost too much. Maybe $10,000 or so."

But when you leave that meeting, you start to realize there's no way you can finish the project in one month. You have already committed to another project. And, to do the job properly, you'll need to pay another person for their help. Chances are, you forgot to add that factor into the equation.

Your best course of action is to tell your client that you'll review all the information and get back to them very soon. Ideally, tell them you'll be in touch the next day.

This allows you to regroup and gather your thoughts. Review your schedule. Go through the budget, and work out the best way to charge and proceed with the project.

There's nothing wrong with taking a day to get back to your client.

When you reply, however, avoid giving a general timeline and fee. Be sure to outline some of the notes from your meeting and how the client's investment will provide them with the results they are looking for.

So, if you ever find yourself feeling pressured to answer your client, take a minute to breathe and make sure you have all the facts before you commit to a timeline and budget.

Another strategy that I have found effective is to quote your client a range. You can say, "You know, Joe, it's going to be somewhere around $75,000 to $100,000 to achieve these goals. Is that what you had in mind?" This approach allows you to quickly assess if the prospective client is on the same page. If they are, great. If not, better to know early on so you can address the issue without wasting time.

Checklist: Consulting Fees and Pricing

☐ I've figured out how much I want to make each year.

☐ I understand the different kinds of fee structures available to me.

☐ I've thought about how to bring value-based fees into my business.

☐ I understand the benefit of setting up a consulting retainer option

☐ I will put together a Pricing Plan sheet to offer my clients.

☐ I will seriously consider increasing my fees.

☐ I understand the danger of taking equity over cash as payment.

☐ I understand the pitfalls of feeling pressured to make a pricing decision.

CHAPTER 6:
EFFECTIVE CONTRACTS AND PROPOSALS

The Easiest and Most Effective Way to Make Contracts and Proposals Work

Both contracts and proposals are important parts of almost every consulting project. To some, they are a necessary evil. To others, they are too bothersome to spend time on and seem like they offer little real value.

Every consultant has their own favorite style of contract or proposal. There is little benefit to try and cover every possible detail that these documents might include, because each project requires different terms and information.

What we will cover is exactly what you need to know to make this part of your business not only easy, but also effective and valuable to both you and your clients.

It's Not About Length

Having consulted for companies in over twenty industries, I can tell you, no one wants to read a long, drawn-out contract or proposal. Nine times out of 10, such documents will only cause you more problems.

There are instances where 40-plus page proposals and contracts are needed, usually for government work or large-scale bidding projects. There's a lot of business to be had by bidding on government projects. I've been involved in the process a couple of times, but I'm far from an expert. That being the case, we won't cover this area in great detail. If you want more information on this, let me know, and I'll point you in the right direction.

Now, back to the proposals and contracts you'll use in most situations.

In my business, I use a combined proposal and contract. It's usually two pages, but sometimes stretches to three. Here's why: most proposals that go on and on for pages contain 30 percent or so real meat, and the rest is just re-used fluff. Consultants try to use the proposal to do all the selling, and it comes off sounding like a used car salesman.

Clients aren't stupid. They don't need to hear every detail about your company all over again. Remember, by this point, you have already met with them, discussed the value you can bring and how you can help them solve their problem.

The proposal and contract shouldn't be used to persuade a prospective client to become an actual client. By the time you deliver them these documents, they should already be sold on you. You should have already engaged in a sales conversation and received the go-ahead.

So, what are these documents for? The proposal is used to outline what you will do during the project. It's broken down into easy-to-read and digestible chunks of information. Its purpose is to show the client on paper the steps you will be taking during the project to help them achieve the result you've already discussed.

Don't Waste Your Time

Consultants who create proposals and send them all over town whenever someone asks for an estimate are just wasting their time.

Again, the proposal shouldn't do the selling. That's your job, and you can only do that by meeting with the prospective client. Only when they've shown you that they are genuinely interested in moving forward should you send a proposal.

By this time, the client should have already asked you what your fee is or how much the project is going to cost, and you should have already told them what to expect. The proposal's job is to distill the conversation you and the prospective client have had so that both of you are on the same page.

Most problems in consulting projects are caused by a lack of communication. That generally begins when the client expects something different than what the consultant is delivering.

The proposal helps to solve this problem. Because both parties are clear and have shown their understanding of what will be provided during the project, including issues such as payment, time to be spent on the project, and so on.

What Your Proposal Should Cover

The purpose of your proposal is not to win business, but rather, to seal the deal. The business should have already been won when you met with your client. The reason you are providing the proposal and agreement is to clarify and re-state the issue that your client is facing and that you will help to solve.

Avoid including new information, because confusion on the part of the buyer leads to inaction. By now, your client will have already told you what their challenge is and how they need your help. If you've done your job properly, you should have already qualified your client and confirmed that they understand the range of financial investment that is required for the project.

You won't have given them an exact number yet, but rather a ballpark figure to ensure they are serious and that you are both playing on the same field. If you're tempted to include information that hasn't already been discussed with the client, ask yourself, "Is there value for my buyer to see this in the proposal now?" If not, cut it out.

Your proposal acts as a final review of why the client will engage your expertise, so it is only fitting that your proposal be married to an agreement so that, once your client confirms that everything you've talked about and agreed to is clear on both sides, the project can begin. There is no need to provide a separate proposal and agreement.

Below, you will find the components of the most effective proposal. When writing your proposal, stick to professional and easy-to-understand language. Avoid overcomplicated legalese. A conversational tone is fine; however, it is preferable that it reads like a strong and solid professional document. Remember, the buyer should already know what to expect by this point, so don't include any surprises.

Components of a Successful Proposal and Agreement

Project Overview

The Project Overview section is where you provide context for the project. This section isn't meant to go into details of your client's company and history. Instead, use this as an opportunity to re-state the problem that you, as their consultant, will help to solve.

The project overview should be kept concise and to the point. Generally, one or two paragraphs give ample room to review the issue and how you and your client have agreed that you will help solve it.

Goals

The Goals section of your proposal and agreement is where you define the goals for this project. You don't have to get too specific. Sometimes, by making them too specific, you are held to numbers that are unattainable due to changes in the project.

More often, if you make the goals too specific and low, everyone who is buying into the project on the client side might aim too low. You want people to aim for the stars. That said, if you set the goals too high and unrealistically, you will regret it later as they come back to bite you when your client says you didn't reach the overzealous goals you set.

Your goals can be listed as bullet points and might look like this:

- Increase sales compared to last year.

- Improve the company's website conversion rate.

- Reduce time to market by at least 25%.

Don't worry about listing every single possible goal. Just include the main goals that are most critical to the project and that your client cares about most.

Success Metrics

The Success Metrics section of your proposal and agreement is critical. This is where you re-state what you and your client have agreed things will look like when the project has been completed successfully.

What outcomes can your client expect to see? What will have changed? Clearly defining this gives you and your client a specific target to aim for and makes it clear when the project should end.

For this section, include things like: "your cost per lead will have decreased significantly," "the company will have an established set of brand guidelines to follow," and "you will receive more than double the publicity than the previous year."

Return on Investment

While the success metrics explain what you and your client will look for to ensure the successful completion of the project, the Return on Investment section assigns a value to it.

To better help your client justify spending good money on bringing you in as their consultant, here is where you can demonstrate how much value you will add to their business.

For example, you might state how much money you will help them make or save over the next 6 to 12 months. Maybe your work will lead to a manufacturing process or system being more efficient and faster, resulting in an additional $300,000 to your client's bottom line.

The value you add to each project will be different and will depend on each client. However, it should be a significant return on investment in order for your client to rationalize their need to hire you.

Options

Once you've established the Goals, Success Metrics, and Return on Investment, it's time to give your client some options. We discussed this in the section on pricing, though it is worthwhile to review it again in the context of proposals and agreements.

Proposals that provide clients with only one option experience a much higher rejection rate. As I said before, taking this route is essentially like telling to your client, "It's my way or the highway." To which most of them will respond, "No thanks."

Offering clients two options is far better. However, if your client doesn't like either of the options, your chances of sealing the deal are slim.

Research indicates that providing your client with three options is the best way to go. Offer a basic, standard, and advanced package to meet a range of needs. Give them interesting names, such as the Bronze, Gold, and Platinum plans.

Each option you provide your client should add more value than the one before. You can also give optional components or services that can be added on to any package to provide more value.

Not only will you provide more value in each subsequent option, you should also increase the fee. In general, more value = bigger fee. Beside each option, you may choose to list the price, which I prefer to call the "investment."

Some consultants include the fee beside each option, so it's easy for the client to associate the cost with each specific package. Other consultants place the fees for each option in the Terms section of the proposal and agreement, so that clients don't focus on the price when looking at each option. Instead, they decide which option suits their needs the best.

Responsibilities

The Responsibilities section is often left out of proposals. While much of the content might seem like common knowledge, you need to state it. If an issue arises during the project, like your client doesn't respond to you promptly, it is in the project's best interest that both can refer to what you agreed upon.

In this section, clarify what you, the consultant, are in charge of and what you expect from your client. For you, this could be things like providing a summary report at the end of each week, keeping all information your client shares with you confidential, letting your client know about any changes in the timeline of the project, and responding to emails and calls within 24 hours.

Your client's responsibilities might include things like making payment within seven days of invoice, responding to your emails or calls within one business day, providing access to all documents and company information needed for the project, paying all out-of-pocket expenses, assigning someone from the client company to support you throughout the project, and so on.

Guarantee

While some consultants choose to bury their guarantee in the Terms section of their proposal and agreement, I believe it deserves more attention. Stating your guarantee in its own section communicates that your guarantee is strong; you're proud of it and not afraid to stand behind it.

Your guarantee can mention that if you fail to complete the project on time and within budget, you will provide an additional service at no cost. Or maybe you guarantee that if you fail to achieve the results you and your client have agreed to, you will continue to work for your client at no cost until those results have been achieved. The purpose of your guarantee is to reduce, and where possible, remove any risk that your client may feel about hiring you for the project.

Terms

The Terms section is where you list the start and projected end date of the project. You can also use this section to include information on how you want to receive payment, whether a deposit is required, and if payment should be made at certain times throughout the project.

As discussed in the Options section, if you've decided not to include your fee (your client's investment for each option), then you should clearly label the cost for each option here.

Any other information you wish to include about the project, possible cancelation or termination fees, or clauses can also be included here.

However, a word of warning, the more complicated you make this part of your proposal and agreement, the greater the chance your client will get stuck on something or will want input from other people.

It is always best to include only what you feel is necessary. Everything else should be left out. Keep it straightforward and to the point.

Signatures

This is the final part of your proposal and agreement. Here you want to list the date that the document is signed.

As with most official agreements, include your company's name, your name, your client's company name, and your client's name. Below each, you should leave room for both of your signatures.

You can also include contact information and any instructions on how you want your client to send the document back to you, whether you would like it to be faxed to a specific number or emailed to a certain address.

Before sending the document to your client, be sure to sign it. That way as soon as your client signs the agreement and sends it back to you, there is nothing left to do but get started on the project.

If you're like most consultants, you may be leaving a lot of money on the table with your proposals.

Use our Consultant Proposal Template to help you write irresistible proposals—and win more business.

**Grab a copy of the template and make your proposal writing more effective and efficient
consultingsuccess.com/bookbonus**

Checklist: Contracts and Proposals

☐ I will pre-sell my clients during a face-to-face meeting and let my proposal complete the deal.

☐ I understand the value of making my proposal easy to digest.

☐ I will avoid including new information in the proposal.

☐ I know and understand what the key components of an effective proposal are.

☐ My proposal and contract/agreement for clients is simple and effective.

CHAPTER 7:
CLIENT DEVELOPMENT FOR CONSULTANT

The Value of Networking

S ome people are natural networkers. They have strong people skills and love getting into conversations. They are outgoing, so networking is easy.

If you're not one of those people—I wasn't always—then you'll need to make an extra effort. Networking is, without question, one of the best ways to grow your business.

These days, most cities offer weekly events that span a wide range of industries and interests. Find something that fits your area of expertise.

If you live in a small town and don't have access to these kinds of offline events, you can begin your networking online. Get active on sites where you can interact with other members. These might include social networking sites, blogs, and other communities.

The Two Main Types of Networking

There are two main kinds of networking.

1. Building Skills:

The first is networking to build your skills. Here your goal is to surround yourself with others in the same industry as yourself or who share the same goal.

Opportunities include meetings, events, and online communities for consultants in specific areas like PR, marketing, social media, and management. Or you can network where people come from different industries but all have the same goal in mind. For example, marketing groups, self-development meetings, and so on.

All of these are good ways to meet other people with similar goals and interests.

This kind of networking helps you build your skills, and introduces you to new ideas, strategies, and techniques that are working for others.

2. Building Business:

The second type, and just as important, is networking with the goal of building business. Opportunities include events, seminars, and other programs that your ideal clients attend.

Remember, you want to be wherever your clients are.

The mistake most people make at these events is that they take a short-term view of relationship building and business generation. That is, they only attend these kinds of events when they are actively looking for new business. As a result, they come in pushing to make something happen. It's unnatural, and prospective clients can smell it a mile away.

Networking isn't about instant results. Far from it. Sure, there are cases where I've gone to a business event and walked away with a new client, but that seldom happens.

If you want to make the most of your networking, try attending industry events rather than "networking" events.

Think about associations, organizations, seminars, and presentations that your clients or potential strategic partners would attend. They often cost a bit of money. Not much, but enough to weed out the tire kickers.

You'll find that the people who go to these events are there to learn, not just to network. Consequently, they tend to be more genuine. The way you meet them will be more real, and you'll find starting a relationship with people much easier.

Here's the thing—networking is extremely powerful, but it takes time. If you go into an event expecting to walk away with new business, you'll likely be disappointed.

Nevertheless, walk in with a plan to meet potential clients or partners and build relationships with them over time. Do that, and you'll start seeing results.

The more events you attend, the more relationships you start. The more connections you create, assuming you maintain them, (very important that you do), the more opportunities you'll find yourself being presented with.

The goal of business networking is to create genuine relationships. These take time to develop, but they also pay a big return down the road.

Give, Give, and You Shall Receive

The idea that since you're attending a business networking event you should receive some instant benefit is like thinking that you deserve to win the lottery because you bought a ticket.

The most powerful principle in networking is the act of giving. When you walk around the room and introduce yourself to people, your job is to find out about them, not to spend the time talking about yourself.

It's definitely a good idea to let each person you meet know what it is you do and give them your business card. After that, start asking (or start off by asking) what it is that they do. Try to find out about their business and what challenges they experience.

Your goal should be finding ways that you can help the people you meet. The more people you help by sharing information with them or referring business to them or making other introductions, the more you'll get out of the relationship. Here's why:

Consulting Success

When someone is kind to you, when they give you something out of the kindness of their heart, don't you feel the need to reciprocate? To give them something in return? Most people do. This is a very powerful approach, because the more people you meet and the more you give, the more will come back to you in return.

Getting Attention and Interest

So, you've decided to attend a networking event. You know the goal is to build more relationships, and you understand this takes time. How should you go about introducing yourself? What can you say to get people's attention?

Some call this the Elevator Pitch. The idea is to imagine you're riding an elevator with a prospective client. You have 10 to 30 seconds. How can you get their attention and interest? What should you say?

Here's a formula you can use:

What Kinds of Companies You Work With + The Result You Get for Clients + What Makes You Different

For example:

"I work with technology companies and help them increase their sales leads while reducing their advertising costs. Plus, my clients only pay me when they get results."

I know, it sounds kind of corny, but it works. You have to remember that you're not just walking up to someone and saying this without any context.

Usually, you'll meet someone, exchange names, and talk about the event or some other general topic. At some point in the conversation, hopefully after you've been politely asking about their business, they will ask you what it is that you do. That's when you start telling them.

Let's break down the above formula and explain why it works:

What Kinds of Companies You Work With: Companies want specialists. By starting off telling them you work with companies in their industry, it shows you already have some experience and an understanding of what's important to them.

The Result You Get for Clients: Most people don't care how big or small you are, not right away. What they care about are results, so tell them what your end game is—why companies hire you and how you can help them.

What Makes You Different: "Okay, so you're a management consultant. Great! There are a million others who do the same thing as you. What makes you different?" That's what goes through a business owner's mind. Cut through that objection and arouse interest by telling them how you are different and why they should care.

This is a simple formula. If you take a few minutes to write down some ideas for yourself and then start practicing them at the next networking event you attend, you'll be impressed with the results.

In fact, the statement you create from this formula can be used in any situation when someone asks you what it is that you do, especially when it comes to getting referrals. Let's jump into that next.

Secrets to Getting Referrals

A sk any successful consultant how they get their clients, and more than 90 percent of them will tell you they come from referrals.

A referral is when someone, whether a friend, family member, acquaintance, or client, refers another prospective client to you.

They do this because they care for you, respect you, trust you, or know you can get the job done to provide results. Sometimes, it's all of these reasons combined.

By far the biggest reason is that a past or current client is satisfied with the work you've done for them, and when someone asks if they know of anyone who can help them with their PR, marketing, or management, your name is the one that comes up.

Referrals are not only the most common way of receiving business, they are also the most effective and the cheapest.

They are the most effective since you have to do much less to sell the new client, because the referrer has already done most of it for you. And since they are not part of your company, they are more credible. Remember, external endorsements from satisfied customers are always more credible than anything you can say. This means each referral has a layer of trust built in, helping you close a sale more quickly.

They are the cheapest because in most cases, you don't have to spend a great deal of money on marketing to get referrals.

How to Get Referrals

The best way to get referrals is to be extremely specific about the kinds of referrals you want.

In my second or third year as a consultant, after returning from consulting with companies in Asia, I went around and met with numerous business owners and successful entrepreneurs. I was hungry for information, so I asked family and friends if they knew of anyone I could meet with who might be interested in my services. This was a good move because I spoke my mind and let it be known that I was looking for referrals.

This led to several introductions and meetings. At some point during each meeting, the business person I met with would say, "So what can I do to help you? What kinds of clients are you looking for?" I always replied by saying, "I've worked with companies in many different industries, from technology and financial services to pharmaceutical and more. I'd be happy to work with any kind of company."

I was covering all my bases, right? Wrong. This kind of reply got me nowhere. The business owners were willing to help, but I made their offer a hard one to fulfill.

I wasn't giving any guidance or pointing them in the direction I wanted to go. I wasn't targeting the specific type of referral I wanted. The business owners were left trying to scan through every company they knew, a number in the hundreds or thousands. Their brains were getting overloaded with information. The result was a complete shutdown with no referral given.

Once I understood my mistake, I went to my next few meetings with a more focused list of the kind of companies I wanted to work with. The results were completely different. I had made the offer an easy one to fulfill.

Based on our conversation and the kind of clients I wanted to work with, business owners were able to list a few companies that fit the criteria.

Developing Your Referral Criteria

To narrow down your criteria, imagine your ideal client.

- What size is their company? (think revenue and employee count)

- What industry are they in?

- Where are they located?

- What kind of corporate culture do they have?

Using these criteria, focus on the kinds of companies you want to be introduced to. That way, every time you meet with someone, you can ask them if they know anyone who fits the bill.

Doing this makes it much easier to receive referrals. The more specific you can be the better.

A Quick and Easy Referral Strategy That Works

If you infrequently ask your friends, family, and clients for referrals, that's exactly what you'll get - infrequent referrals. However, if you put together a more formal referral strategy, you'll get a frequent flow of fresh referrals to grow your business.

One of the simplest and most effective ways to do this is by developing an incentive program and offering it to all of your clients.

The program rewards your clients for any referrals they send you. This concept, also called an affiliate program, is used successfully by many companies. Too few consultants use this, but the ones who do see huge growth in their business.

To make this work, continually make your clients aware of the program. Mention it in your newsletter and any other communications you send to your clients. It's also good to remind your clients about it in meetings.

With this type of program, you reward your clients every time they refer someone to you. The reward could be a discount, a gift certificate, a trip, cash, or any other type of incentive you think they would like

There should be no exceptions for this. Every time you receive a referral, show your appreciation and give thanks. If you don't, you likely won't continue to receive referrals. People want to know that what they are doing is appreciated.

Take a couple of these referral strategies and implement them in your business. Use all of them on an ongoing basis and get ready for a stream of new clients. But remember, referrals don't always come with the turn of a tap. Take a long-term approach and understand that once your system is in place, you'll be well on your way to great success.

The Biggest Factor in Getting New Clients

Hands down, the easiest way to get more clients is to show them you can get results that matter to their business.

The streets are lined with consultants who talk about what they do, but ask them to show how they have delivered measurable results to their clients' businesses in one form or another, and you'll hear nothing but excuses.

That's why you need to become a consultant who can demonstrate results. As soon as you do, everything about your consulting business will improve. Clients will accept what you say more quickly, they'll want to start projects sooner, and they'll refer you to others more often.

If you don't have experience getting results, your first job is to figure out how to do this.

You can take a lower paying project or do some pro-bono work. Do whatever you need to do in order to prove you can generate results!

Something that will definitely help you land more business is removing the risk clients feel about working with you. You do this by offering a guarantee that shows your confidence in the product or service you provide. The stronger your guarantee, the more you diminish the risk your prospective client feels when deciding whether or not to work with you.

Scared that people might actually take you up on your guarantee? Let me give you two thoughts on this. First, fewer people than you imagine will ever ask for a refund, or whatever you're offering in your guarantee, especially if you're any good at what do. Second, if you're not confident in what you're offering, it's a good opportunity to ask yourself if you have the right offer in the first place?

When I first started writing about the importance of consultants offering guarantees to their clients, the market was wide open. Hardly anyone was doing it. Things have changed. These days, practically every business offers a guarantee.

I'll show you how to offer a guarantee in a way that differentiates you in the marketplace and lands new consulting clients and projects.

Well-known online marketer Glenn Livingston said it best (and he may have been quoting someone else), "A REAL guarantee in today's day and age should be so strong it makes you feel like throwing up."

In order to stand out in the marketplace, your guarantee needs to be so strong, so differentiated, that it completely eliminates all the risk a prospective client might feel. They need to think and feel, "I have nothing to lose."

The guarantee should focus on what your clients care about. Don't simply guarantee some aspect of your business your clients don't value.

Keep the guarantee straightforward. The more complex you make it, the less powerful it becomes. You want a buyer to understand it right away.

Promote your guarantee. Don't keep it hidden. It can provide you with great marketing leverage. Ensure that you're doing regular check-ins and reviews with your client to stay on top of the project and catch any potential issues before they arise.

Some consultants worry that guarantees are risky and choose not to offer them. The main concern is that each project comes with variables that are out of their control, which means even if they do their best and perform their work flawlessly, the project might still not be completed on time.

Here's the thing. A guarantee is a two-way agreement you make with your client. If your guarantee states that you will complete the project on time and on budget every time, ensure that you also state this is based on the client keeping up with their responsibilities and the agreed upon timeline.

Don't guarantee something you can't control.

Risk breeds hesitation. Hesitation creates procrastination. None of those make you money. Removing the risk does. Make your guarantee specific and meaningful, but make it a two-way agreement. Communicate your confidence in it, and watch your sales grow.

Leveraging Partnerships to Find New Clients

Before I dive into more ways of landing new clients through marketing, let's discuss an often-overlooked area: partnerships.

As a consultant, you'll spend a good deal of your time working alone, but it doesn't have to be that way. By establishing relationships with other like-minded professionals in industries that complement yours, you open a gateway to many more project opportunities. These professionals could include designers, illustrators, print shops, programmers, copywriters, finance experts, or other marketing people.

Collaborating with others on projects can work many ways, and if you approach it correctly, you can benefit from all of them.

1. You're Central:

In this situation, you bring on another professional to offer additional services to your clients that you otherwise couldn't.

By doing this, your client gets more value since the other professional is a specialist, and you look better as you're providing effective services to your clients. But it gets better than that.

Let's use the example of a marketing consultant who gets paid on an hourly basis. In this case, they are charging their client $100/hour. The client needs a new website designed, so the marketing consultant contacts a web developer he knows and offers him $75 an hour to develop the site. The marketing consultant tells the client how many hours they estimate it will take, and the client agrees.

Since it's your project and you're the one meeting and dealing with the client, you keep an extra $25/hour—the difference between what you're making and what you're paying the web developer. So not only are you providing your client with more value, you're also making more money in the process. A win-win for everyone.

2. They're Central:

Using the example of the marketing consultant and web developer, let's look at another way this relationship can benefit both people. The web developer who also acts as a website consultant has several clients. One of them happens to need help with their marketing strategy. Who do you think the web developer/consultant calls to bring into the mix? The marketing consultant, of course.

Now the pricing might be opposite. The web developer/consultant might take 10 to 15 percent of the marketing consultant's fee, as he's the one who made the introduction.

The actual amount taken depends on the involvement. If they are just introducing you and stepping away, they'd get less. If they are going to be the main point of contact for the client throughout and handle all payments, they'd get more.

3. Both Central:

In this final example of how to make partnerships work, the marketing consultant and web developer decide to team up and try to win new client business together. They share the responsibilities, but each brings their own experience and skills to the table.

The value in this is that, sometimes, larger companies that have big projects don't want to deal with an individual consultant, so they are more likely to award the project when they see a team behind it.

Regardless of which of these three partnerships approaches you take (maybe you'll try them all), it should be clear that this is a great way to build your business. This should also demonstrate to you the importance of relationships, which are usually built through networking.

None of this will happen overnight, but if you're out networking, asking for referrals, and connecting with like-minded people, great things usually start coming together.

Host-Beneficiary Strategy

Jay Abraham, one of the leading marketing minds of our time, teaches an extremely powerful marketing strategy called the host-beneficiary.

Let me give you an example of how it works.

You run a yoga studio (or you consult for one). You want to increase your number of customers and sales, yet you have a limited budget.

Here's what you do. You know your massage therapist runs a thriving practice. You speak to him and ask him if he'd be interested in making a few thousand dollars extra without having to do much of anything.

How can that be?

You propose to your massage therapist that you'll put together a letter that offers his patients a superb discount on yoga and meditation classes to help them manage stress and improve their well-being.

You'll put together the letter, the envelope, and the postage. The only thing your therapist has to do is provide the mailing labels of his clients.

You'll send them out, and for every person that signs up, you'll give your therapist $100.

As a result of mailing to 800 clients, you get 100 people to sign up. You pay your therapist $10,000, and you're happy because you know the lifetime value of each client is, on average, four months at $100/month.

The host-beneficiary strategy can be applied in almost every industry.

Follow Up and Be Persistent

Maybe it's because of the society we live in today. Ads online claiming, "I made $3,000 last month working only two hours at home in my pajamas," have become more common than printed newspapers.

I have no problem with everything going digital and mobile. What I find sad is the number of people who expect everything to work instantly for them.

New consultants do a little bit of marketing, see that it's not working, and give up, moving on to the next thing that has to work better for them because this one clearly didn't.

It's understandable. These days information is freely available and accessible 24/7 at a click of the mouse or the touch of a screen.

The reality, however, is that marketing successes are rarely instant.

Marketing requires continuous and consistent effort. It takes an average of seven "touches" to turn a lukewarm prospect into a customer.

Let's look at a few common situations:

- You run one ad, and it doesn't work, so you call it quits.

- You send out an email, then make one follow up call. They are too busy to talk with you, so you never contact them again.

- You receive a request for information. You send that information yet never follow up to see how you can help the prospect.

These are just a few of the many situations consultants find themselves in, and the unfortunate and most likely result is that no business gets booked.

Why? Because there was no ongoing follow up. No system. No campaign. All of these are like taking salt and pepper and shaking them blindly around your kitchen, hoping that some of it will land in the frying pan. A little might, but most won't.

Several years ago, I met the owner of a professional services firm at a business lunch. We got to talking, and he asked me what I did. I told him I worked with business owners to help improve their marketing and bring in more leads for their businesses. He was interested and said that he could use some help.

Good start and a worthwhile lunch, I thought.

Consulting Success

I later found out that another person I knew at that lunch had actually told this business owner about my work and put in a few good words. They had already started to grease the wheels for me, even though I didn't know it.

Sounds like a simple story about landing another client, right? Wrong. There's much more to this story. After this business owner and I talked, I told him I'd be in touch. There was too much good food and drink and too many others to talk to, so we said our goodbyes, and the day went on.

The next day, I sent the business owner an email and let him know we could set up a time to meet. I didn't receive a reply.

A couple of days passed and still nothing. A week later, I sent him another email. Still no reply.

For many new to the consulting business, this can be a time when you get down on yourself. After that initial talk, you're excited at the prospect of landing a new client.

But it doesn't work like that.

You quickly learn that a new client is not a new client until you've deposited their check in the bank.

Never count your chickens before they hatch. It's too painful and emotionally draining to get all excited about something that has yet to materialize.

That's why I wasn't overly concerned that I wasn't hearing back. Besides, I had plenty of other business going on already.

It took another couple of emails over the course of a month before we scheduled our first meeting.

I picked up the phone one day and got hold of the business owner. Many people would have expected him to be annoyed by my constant nagging. However, to me that's called follow up.

And guess what happened?

He said, "Michael, thanks for calling and not giving up on me. I've been so busy but wanted to get together and talk about our marketing."

Another time, one of my companies started work on expanding the number of partnerships we had with other large organizations. There was one in particular that I wanted to go after

Contact was initiated. I called them, and they expressed interest. However, they didn't make it easy. Although they expressed interest, I found it hard to close the deal.

Ten emails went back and forth. A couple more calls across the country. Then ten more emails. Promises were made and broken.

My business partner told me to drop it, and I learned many years ago that he was probably right. In many cases, you have to be careful not to dig yourself deeper into a hole. But in this situation, I had a feeling I could make this happen, so I persisted.

Fifty-seven emails later, I was getting very close. In fact, I was told the brass had given the deal the go-ahead. I wouldn't believe it until I saw it. A couple of days later, I got an email. It was official.

Consulting Success

Looking back, there's no way this deal would have gotten done if I hadn't had patience and persistence. If I had given up after the thirtieth email, I wouldn't have landed this great new client.

If the deal had been small, I wouldn't have spent so much time on it. But 57 emails and many calls later, the deal was successfully completed.

It's simple. Always follow up.

Don't call every day. Don't get all worked up. Just make a note in your schedule to continually follow up with people who have shown interest in working with you. You're going to love the positive impact this will have on your business.

When your marketing doesn't produce the results you're after, don't give up and call it a day. Every failure (if you want to call it that) can be and should be turned into a lesson.

Ask yourself: What can be improved? Why didn't that work? What can I change?

The more effort and focus you put on your marketing, the more you'll get out of it!

More than 80% of sales are won after 5+ follow-ups — and most consultants give up after the first try. We've built a Follow-Up Spreadsheet Tracker so you can keep yourself accountable.

Join the 20% of the consultants winning 80% of the business by tracking your follow-ups using our spreadsheet at consultingsuccess.com/bookbonus

---

Getting More out of Existing Clients

Adding new clients isn't the only focus of client development. A great way to generate more business for your consulting practice is to get more out of your existing client base.

An effective way to do this is to constantly study your clients' business.

The more aware you are of what challenges they face, the better prepared you'll be to offer new approaches and solutions to their problems.

Let's say your client has a new workshop coming up. Maybe you can help them with the setup, registration, marketing, or follow up, depending on what your expertise is.

Before the holiday season approaches, you can speak to your client about a new idea you have for a special promotion.

Some consultants choose not to take this approach. They don't want to take on client work unless it's directly related to their area of expertise. That's fine.

But remember, you can outsource this additional work, bringing in other experts to do the work, while you still take a commission or finder's fee. You can also use this opportunity to build the skills of your company so you can offer the additional services to other clients.

Most independent consultants don't need more than five to ten clients a year. There are plenty of opportunities to help your existing clients do more and do it better than they could without you. Your job is to simply help them find those opportunities and then capitalize on them.

Always be on the lookout for new opportunities.

Challenges with Client Development

You might run into a few snags when you're trying to generate new clients. Here are a few things to be aware of.

Identifying the True Buyer

You think you've just landed a new consulting client. You met the marketing coordinator at a medium-sized company, and she told you that she's talked to her boss about you and they are interested in your services. You're feeling good.

The next week you go to this company's office to sit down and get things going. The marketing coordinator greets you in the reception area. She takes you into a conference room and closes the door.

She begins asking questions about your skills. "What can you do for the company? How much will you charge for your services? My boss also wanted me to ask—"

Do you see anything wrong with this scenario?

155

I hope so, because there certainly is. This consultant has entered into a project that is sure to present several challenges. It'll likely turn into a project that the consultant regrets taking on once it gets started.

Why?

Because the consultant has made one big mistake—they've failed to identify the "true buyer."

The true buyer is not the marketing coordinator. It is often not even the manager. It can really only be the person who is writing the checks or making the final decisions on whether or not the consultant will get paid. Who is this person? It's the owner, the partner, the CEO, or the President.

As a consultant, if you're not dealing directly with the person who calls the shots, you're wasting your time.

Most of us have been in situations like this at one time or another. You put a lot of effort into a project only to feel like you're getting spun in circles by the client. The main reason this happens is because you are not speaking directly with the decision maker. Identify who the decision maker is at the company, and then make sure you meet with them. Take them out for lunch. Get to know them. Build a relationship with them.

They are the ones who you need to please, the ones who make the decisions. The ones who will sign their name on the check that gets you paid.

Too many consultants fail to meet with the true buyer. Save yourself time and stress by ensuring you do.

Tons of Leads, No Actual Business

It's not uncommon for consultants and independent professionals to find their pipeline full of leads and prospective business, though not enough of that business gets closed.

Imagine a funnel being filled with small marbles from the wide end at the top. Each one represents a potential client and project. You know that the majority of these should be coming out the bottom in the form of a sale, yet nothing moves.

When you find yourself in this situation, it is important to analyze the contributing factors. Often, one or more issues are at play. Once you deal with the issues, it's like you've greased up the marbles, and they start coming out of the bottom at a quick rate.

Here are several strategies to help you identify the problem in your sales cycle to fix it and grow your business:

Houston, We Have a Problem

In fact, you might have more than one. However, it's not a problem with *your* business. It might be a problem your prospective client is facing. Once you've identified it, you can ensure that you focus your language and communications to address it.

To uncover what's really going on and how big the problem is, consultant and author Andrew Sobel suggests asking questions like: "What is this costing you right now?"; "If you don't fix this problem, what will the consequences be?"; "What do you think this opportunity is worth to your organization?"; "What other issue is this causing you?"; and "Would you say this is one of your top two or three priorities?"

As soon as you've discovered the real issue and what it's worth to your prospective client, you will be well on your way to moving the sales cycle along.

Clear a Path

Neglecting to outline the steps involved in the sales process clearly for the client is a mistake many consultants make. At the end of every meeting, you need to inform the client what the next step is and when it will happen. In addition, it helps to walk them through a step-by-step of what your sales process is.

You can start with an analysis, and then transition to a review meeting, then a recommendation session with discussion on investment and so on. The better your prospective client understands your process, the more likely they will be to follow it.

You Are the Authority

Consultants often deal with questions about their authority. If a prospective client doesn't have full trust in you, they will find it very difficult to engage you. In fact, this is one of the key reasons sales cycles can take so long. If the client is not convinced that you're clearly the best option, they will put off making a purchase.

In this situation, you need to do all you can to educate and provide value to your prospective client to prove to them that you are an authority, that you get results, and that they can trust you. Think about case studies, testimonials, reports, and demonstrations.

Shrink the Table

If you've ever sat a boardroom table and had a feeling that too many people are present, you know what I'm getting at with this point. When you are moving a prospective client through the sales cycle, it's critical that you speak directly with the decision maker.

Anyone who doesn't need to be there ideally shouldn't be. If they can add value to the conversation and process, then value their input and attendance. If not, focus your energy on speaking directly with the decision maker. You will find that as soon as you talk to the right person and get on the same page with them, the whole sales cycle will speed up.

Eliminate Objections

Sometimes asking a simple question can provide you with extremely powerful information. For example, "What would we need to have ready in order for us to start this project at the beginning of next month?" The goal here is to figure out what your prospective client's real objections are. You can then figure out how to remove those objections and create a clear route to win the project.

Why Rush?

If there is no scarcity involved, then your prospective client has no reason to move quickly. Scarcity doesn't have to be a limited-time offer. It can be something as simple as, "We can only accept two new projects next month, so if you want to do this soon, it would be best to get moving quickly."

Or scarcity can be focused more on the company. "How much is this issue costing your company each day it is not dealt with?" If it's a big problem, finding a solution and having it implemented ASAP becomes valuable.

By looking at your current sales cycle and your prospective client and referencing each of these points, you'll be able to uncover the current roadblocks in your path, remove them, and be well on your way to closing more sales.

Ten Things Clients Hate and How to Avoid Them

Andrew Sobel, well-respected consultant and author, wrote an article on "Things Clients Hate." The lessons he shared are so valuable I wanted to list the top ten, along with my notes on each. I discuss several of these throughout the book, but this can be a good checklist for your business.

1) **A generic approach** – When you approach a client, provide them information about your consulting services and how you can help them. Do you customize it for them, or are you reusing your materials? If the latter, this might come off as generic to your clients and doesn't show them you care about THEIR business.

2) **Overselling** – Being eager and determined to work hard and to land more consulting clients is good. Trying to push a sale on the first meeting with a prospective client is bad. Get to know your prospect before you try to sell them.

3) **Long slide decks** – Do I really need to say much about this? Keep your presentations short and to the point. Make them visual and keep them light on text. Check out presentations by Guy Kawasaki or Seth Godin for great examples.

4) **Wanting business immediately** – Similar to number two, yet slightly different. "When you meet with a prospect, you must have a long-term perspective. You must have the attitude that if something works out in the short term, that's great, but if not, that's OK too." says Sobel.

5) **Not respecting their time** – This goes beyond showing up late for client meetings. This is about respecting time in general. Time is a precious commodity. Get into the meeting, say what needs to be said, focus on the goal of the meeting, and get out. Don't let things drag on.

6) **Overreaching** – This is a tough one. The point is to avoid selling services to your client that you're not great at. It opens up room for a bad result, and it can damage your reputation as a professional. The approach I recommend is to align yourself with other experts and to offer and provide your clients with additional services through your alliances. That way you generate more business but keep the quality at expert level through the whole experience.

7) **Surprises** – They're nice on birthdays but generally not in business situations. If there are challenging issues to deal with, don't wait until the last minute to spill the beans and tell your client the bad news. Be proactive and upfront at all times. Clients never like hearing bad news, but they hate hearing it at the last minute. It gives them a reason to doubt you and lose trust in you.

8) **Going over their head** – When you have a disagreement with your client, don't be sneaky and try to climb the ladder to discuss the issue with their boss. I suggest dealing only with the boss so that issues like this don't arise, but if you find yourself working with someone lower on the totem pole, it's in your best interest to work the issue out, and if you're still not able to do it together, Sobel suggests that you go together to speak with the boss.

9) **Making them look bad** – This includes things like deflecting blame for a negative result, missing deadlines, and not communicating well. To sum this point up: be professional!

10) **Not delivering** – I talk a lot about this in the Consulting Success System. Hands down, delivering the result that you and your client agreed on is the most important aspect of any project engagement. You can be a great person, but if you don't deliver, you're giving your client a reason to not need your services anymore. Deliver as you've promised, and you'll start getting referral business and see your business truly take off.

Checklist: Finding Clients

- ☐ I'm attending (or going to attend) networking events.
- ☐ I'll work on building relationships at these events, not only on sales.
- ☐ I understand valuable relationships take time to develop.
- ☐ I'll try to help connect and refer people I meet with others I know.
- ☐ I have an effective elevator pitch and have practiced it.
- ☐ I've developed my referral criteria and will go after more referrals.
- ☐ I understand how to use partnerships to build my business.
- ☐ I understand persistence is necessary and will effectively follow up on connections and referrals.
- ☐ I will focus on ways I can get the most out of existing clients.
- ☐ I will identify my true buyer and issues in my sales cycle that may be causing a lack of clients.
- ☐ I will make a checklist of those things that clients do not like that can cost me business.

CHAPTER 8:
MARKETING CONSULTING SERVICES

Landing Your Ideal Clients

For the majority of consultants starting out, getting a steady stream of clients proves to be the most difficult task. But it doesn't have to be. Nor should it.

It's understandable why this happens. Most consultants don't know where to start. Where can they find the right clients, and what should they say to them to win their business? I'll provide answers to these questions and more in this section of the book.

Are You Prepared?

There are many forms of advertising that can put you in front of thousands of people who are looking for a consultant in your industry. You can use Google AdWords and targeted direct mail to name two. Getting in front of people is the easy part.

Too few consultants give enough time and attention to their own marketing. The more you put into marketing and selling, as long as you are doing the right things, the more you will get out of them.

A friend asked me to meet with his brother-in-law, a businessman turned consultant, to get my take on his business plan.

We arranged to meet at a local coffee shop just over the bridge from my home.

We had a good talk over strong coffee. This man had accomplished a lot. He had worked in many places around world, and he had a good list of clients to his name. Now back in the city, he was pushing hard to make this next chapter of his business a success.

He told me all about his plans. He seemed confident that he had what it took to be successful. He'd done it before, so surely he could do it again, he thought.

I offered him some advice about his marketing plan.

But the next time I ran into him, he was packing it up. Folding his cards. He told me he wanted a full-time job. He couldn't deal with the instability of being a consultant.

I wasn't going to try and convince him otherwise. I could see in his eyes he'd already made up his mind, but I had to know why it didn't work out for him.

As he told me about the actions he'd taken and the challenges he'd faced, one thing became clear. He might have been skilled at what he did, but he wasn't marketing himself and his services enough. He isn't alone. A lack of marketing skills for landing new clients and business is one of the biggest issues consultants face.

If you've ever felt this way, you are not alone. Marketing and selling your services is an essential part of your business.

You must be prepared before you start your marketing activities, because as soon as you make your first contact with a potential client, their impression of you is formed. And if it's not a good one, you'll have a hard time winning back their attention.

So How Can You Be Prepared? Ask Yourself These Questions:

1) Have you defined what makes you different from others in the market?

2) Have you generated results in one form or another that will help you prove your skills?

3) Have you clearly listed the services you can provide, and how they will benefit the client?

4) Do you have an understanding of the industry or concerns that face the companies you are targeting in your market?

5) Can you clearly explain how to price your services and the value you provide that justifies the cost?

6) Are you ready to spend some money? Most consultants don't spend very much on promoting their business. That's fine when you're already established and have a strong presence in the market. But if you don't, you need to be prepared to spend some money on marketing and advertising. It doesn't have to be a lot, but the saying "it takes money to make money" holds true.

These are the kinds of questions you need to answer before you begin your marketing. Otherwise, your attempts will largely go wasted. When prepared, you'll be well-equipped to start conversations with potential clients.

Finding New Clients

The secret to finding new clients is something we've talked about before: Focus.

Avoid trying to market to every industry out there without any real criteria. This shotgun approach rarely provides the results you're after.

Instead, create your list of Dream Clients.

To Create this List, Start by Choosing:

- An industry you want to target

- A location you want to target

- A size of company you want to target (either by employees or revenue)

These three criteria are a great place to start. You can then use a service like SalesGenie.com to get a list of companies that match what you're looking for. Websites that provide company information, like SalesGenie, will also provide you with all the contact information you need to contact your dream clients.

If you're on a strict budget, you can do most of your research online or go to your local library and easily come up with a list of fifty to a hundred companies that you'd consider Dream Clients.

Why would you only choose fifty to a hundred companies and forget about the rest? Because most consultants can't handle working with more than five to ten clients at one time. Do you really need to go after a thousand? Of course not.

In addition, it costs a heck of a lot more to keep marketing to hundreds or thousands of companies on a regular basis.

The Marketing Secret of Seven

D id you notice how I said "on a regular basis?" That's right, the notion that you can send out marketing materials one time to a bunch of companies and land them as paying clients is a myth.

In 90 to 95 percent of cases, your first marketing communications to a prospective client will result in NO new business. In fact, it has been proven that it takes seven or more contacts to turn a potential client into a paying client.

Here are some interesting points of data from consultant and author Grant Hicks.

- 5-10 percent chance of having a person become a client after one contact.

- 10-20 percent chance of having a person become a client after two contacts.

- 20-30 percent chance of having a person become a client after three contacts.

- Most advisors give up after three tries.

- 30-40 percent chance of having a person become a client after four contacts.

- 50-70 percent chance of having a person become a client after five touches.

- Numbers soar after five touches.

- 70-80 percent chance of having a person become a client after six and seven contacts.

- In total, 50-80 percent of all new business developed after the fifth, sixth and seventh touch or contact.

And herein lies the big mistake that most consultants make. They run one ad, do a text or email blast, or send some brochures in the mail, and they expect the phones to start ringing. They usually don't, and the consultant decides that what they've done isn't working, so they give up and either stop marketing or quickly abandon ship. BIG mistake.

Here are a few more interesting facts:

- 40-50 percent of professionals will call once and never call again.

- 25-40 percent will contact a prospect the second time and follow up, and that's it.

- 10-20 percent will contact them three times and stop there.

- 5-10 percent will contact or touch people five times or more before doing business with them and become very successful opening new accounts 70-80 percent of the time and earning in the top 5-10 percent of professionals.

Isn't it a shame that most marketers give up after only 2 or 3 attempts to win new business?

With your Dream Client list in hand, you should create a seven-step campaign to get in front of them. And since you're only focusing on fifty to a hundred companies, the cost of such a campaign becomes much more manageable.

For example, your campaign might look something like this:

1) Send a postcard with an offer for a free report

2) Send another postcard. This time you can change a headline or feature a different benefit of the report.

3) Now, you might send a small package with a little gift or toy in it, something to get their attention. Again, talk about the report or about how you can help them.

4) Maybe they've signed up to get your free report. So now you can send them a follow-up email, thanking them for downloading it.

5) A week later, call to follow up and ask if they have any questions. Try to schedule an appointment to meet with them.

6) Maybe you can offer a free seminar to the company's top employees to demonstrate what you can do for them in an educational way.

7) You could use another email or letter in the mail to follow up again with the suggestion for an appointment.

You're probably thinking that sounds too pushy. It's not. It's called effective marketing. And you might even have to take your effective marketing strategy beyond these seven steps to get business with the client. Because of that, I have included a one-year marketing plan.

Do this with every prospective client you meet and your business will, in my experience, see significant growth.

Winning your dream clients won't happen at random. Use our Dream Client Worksheet to get crystal clear on who your ideal clients are. This will help you find more of them and make your messaging and marketing more effective as a result.

Stop "hoping" to win dream clients — get clear on who they are and begin reaching out to them using the Dream Client Worksheet at consultingsuccess.com/bookbonus

Here is a sample 12-month campaign:

Month 1 – Set up a meeting with a prospective client. After the meeting, follow up with a note on how you enjoyed meeting them. Hint: sending an "it was nice to meet you" note in the mail trumps email every time.

Month 2 – Send an educational newsletter with valuable tips.

Month 3 – Send them an email with a cut-out of an industry article they would find interesting.

Month 4 – Call them to see how things are going, and inquire if you can be of any help. Hint: this isn't a sales call. You are not calling to directly sell anything. Your goal here is to check on them and see if you can be of help or answer any questions they may have.

Month 5 – Highlight a case study of a successful project you recently completed.

Month 6 – Send another newsletter with valuable tips.

Month 7 – Offer an assessment or a critique on a part of their business.

Month 8 – Invite them to a seminar or workshop you're organizing.

Month 9 – Send them an article or blog post that you contributed to in an established publication.

Month 10 – Announce a new service or promotion you are offering.

Month 11 – Send a third newsletter with valuable tips.

Month 12 – Send a case study or results from a recent project or highlight some testimonials from clients.

Your actual marketing materials must be effective, but let's talk more about those in a minute.

If you have effective materials and a strong follow-up process, you'll run circles around other consultants in your industry.

You see, follow-up is the least used and most effective aspect of good marketing.

When you plan your marketing communications and target your Dream Clients, be sure to put together a plan that allows you to have multiple contacts with them.

You might question the effectiveness of follow up, so let me explain why it works so well.

Two Buying Factors

The two largest factors in the buying decisions of companies that would likely be interested in your services are:

1. Trust

When a company hears about you for the first time, they don't know what to think. You may be telling the truth, you may not be. They don't know. The same is true when you meet someone for the first time. You have an impression, but you don't really know what to think until you meet them a second and third time. Only then do you start to feel like you know them.

The same is true in marketing. The more often the companies you're targeting see your ads and other marketing materials, the more familiar you become to them. Once they feel like they can trust you, they will be open to your messages and want to meet with you.

2. Cycles

The second reason is buying cycles. Many companies have set budgets, and they can't spend more money on things if they've already allocated their spending for that period.

So, if you just send them one or two communications and give up, there's a good chance you'll never do business with them.

By continually getting in front of them, not only do you create top-of-mind awareness and help them to trust you, but you're there when the time comes to make their next buying decision.

The Hard Sell Doesn't Work Anymore

In all of your marketing efforts and networking activities, the idea that you need to push the benefits of your business until someone sits up and takes notice isn't as valid as it used to be.

We're all bombarded with advertising messages and have trained our brains to shut down when we see commercials and blatant promotions.

The new way to sell is called the soft sell. Better known as the educational approach. The more you educate people, the more they'll see you as an authority.

The idea of giving out free advice is a hard one for many consultants to swallow. They feel that advice is what they sell and so they shouldn't give it away for free. This way of thinking is understandable, but it's short-sighted.

By opening up and sharing some of your knowledge with people, you'll find yourself surrounded with many more opportunities than if you remain closed.

You see, a prospective client is going to make a purchase at some time. Regardless of what you're selling, at some point, they will need to buy it. And when they do, who do you think they're going to buy from?

The consultant that educates and guides them towards the right decisions without pushing, or the consultant who won't give any valuable advice unless they receive payment for it? The first consultant will find themselves many times richer.

The secret is that you don't need to give away everything you know. In fact, you shouldn't. When a prospective client asks you a question or asks for your advice, you should be happy to share with them your thoughts on the subject.

For example, you can offer a free educational presentation that will provide value, insights, or ideas for the prospective client. You can present this information in a variety of ways, including over the phone, through a social network site, or in person.

Draw a client in by giving them incentive to listen to your information. Tell them that you've been speaking with their competitors (drop a few names) and that you'd like to book a time with them, too. You don't have to have presented to their competitors yet, but saying that you're talking to them will get their attention. If their competitors are going to see this, they'd better see it right away. Plus, it's free!

During the presentation, share with them how you believe you can help them improve their services by tweaking their current operations. Be sure that your presentation is to the point, easy to understand, and gives plenty of data, research findings, and valuable information. Make your point, and tell them what the potential solutions would be.

What you'll find is that they'll see you as an authority. Plus, you will have gotten your foot in the door and made your case. They'll feel like they have received value from you without giving you anything in return, so when they're ready to buy, they'll come right back to you, because they owe you.

What's more, while many potential clients love hearing your take on their situation, when it comes to implementation, they have no clue how to move forward, and most of the time they don't want to do it themselves. They prefer to pay someone else and have them do it properly.

So, don't be too shy to share what you know. The more value you give, the more you will receive.

Creating Marketing Materials That Get Results

Regardless of how often you send out marketing materials, if they are ineffective to start with, you're likely to see little response. Sure, sending out anything on a regular basis is better than nothing, but if you're going to take the time and expense to do so, you'd better make it worth your while.

Here are four key concepts to help you ensure that your marketing gets results:

1. USP

Your USP is your unique selling proposition. Also called your competitive advantage or value proposition. It's typically a short sentence or two about what makes you different from your competitors.

When someone asks why they should choose your consulting services over someone else's, how would you reply? Your USP should highlight your special focus, a guarantee you offer, your experience and/or your results.

Also, what you are offering needs to be something that the market actually believes is valuable, something they'd be willing to pay for and feel strongly enough about to do business with you. The best USPs are memorable and instantly differentiate you from others.

Domino's Pizza's old USP went something like: "Delivered to your door in thirty minutes or you don't pay."

When everyone used to go to video stores to get their movies (remember those days?), Blockbuster had a compelling USP. They guaranteed the latest arrival would be in store, or you wouldn't have to pay for it next time.

Avis car rental used to say, "We're Avis, we're number 2, so we try harder." This played off the fact that another car company was sitting pretty in the number one spot and didn't have as much of a reason as Avis had to win and keep customers' business.

All of these USPs make or imply promises. They are believable, easy to remember, and very effective.

Remember, you can't make a name for yourself by being like every other business in your market. To make my point, allow me to draw on the title of a great book by Jack Trout, *Differentiate or Die*.

Now it's time for you to create your own value proposition. I always like to use a formula for this, which is:

Who Your Customers Are + What You Provide Them + Why They Buy From You

Let's break this down:

- **Who your customers are** - The more you target a group, the more receptive they will be to your message. Rather than saying, "I help companies with their management strategies," think about getting focused and saying something like, "I help technology companies with 50 to 500 employees in the Arizona area to..." Compare those two sentences. Do you see how much more relevant and powerful the second one would be if that was your target audience?

- **What you provide them** - What is it that you do? What is your product or service? When you consider this, again, put yourself in your clients' shoes. Think about the real product or service you are providing that they care about, not what you think is important. Use language that your customers use.

- **Why they buy from you** - This one is critical. What separates you from the competition? This one causes the biggest challenge for most consultants. Why? Because things like "high-quality," "best service," and "lowest price" are not differentiators anymore. Everyone says they have the highest-quality products and great service.

You need to come up with something that sets you apart. Give thought to how you deliver your product or service, your guarantee, or maybe there is some other unique benefit you provide that others don't. It's important to remember that your differentiator doesn't have to be completely unique. Even if your competitor has the same capability as you do, if they are not communicating and promoting that uniqueness, you can take hold of it and own it in the marketplace.

There are two ways I advise consultants to write their value propositions.

1) **The long form.** Take a paragraph or two to answer the three formula questions above in as much detail as you can. Maybe you'll use half a page. You can then edit it down and end up with some great copy that speaks to your ideal clients. You can place that on your website and use it in your advertising.

2) **The short form.** Taking what you've written above, and looking at the formula I mentioned, try to get your value proposition down to a single sentence. This is what you will use when meeting new people to explain what you do.

Place it on your website, business cards, brochures, online ads, voicemail—pretty much anywhere and everywhere you can.

You may be wondering, "How do I know if my value proposition is going to work?" That's a great question.

You can use your value proposition when meeting new people at networking events. You'll quickly be able to see how people respond to you, and based on their response, you can make slight adjustments in your wording.

Another highly effective way to test your value proposition is with Google AdWords. This will cost you, but for $50 to $100 you can usually get some great data. Here's how this works. You put together two to three different variations of your value proposition as ads.

You then run them all at the same time, directing that traffic to your site or a landing page. You will start to see which ads (and corresponding value proposition) are receiving the most clicks and highest CTR. You then know which one speaks to your target audience most effectively.

Put all of this into practice and start enjoying the benefits of standing out in your marketplace, increased leads, and new clients.

2. Benefits

This one is pretty straightforward. Do your marketing materials clearly list the benefits that your Dream Client will receive by working with you? Remember, the benefits are what the client will gain from working with you, not just what you offer.

The better understanding you have of your Dream Clients' industries and their needs, the better you will be able to craft meaningful benefits for your marketing materials.

3. Build Trust

There are several ways you can build trust. The two most popular are to either establish yourself as a credible expert or to show testimonials from satisfied clients and other professionals who have given you praise in the past.

Avoid labeling yourself as a consultant. It's vague, holds little meaning, and certainly won't help you in landing clients. People don't hire you because you are a consultant. They hire you because you're an expert in something. On the flip side, simply labeling yourself an expert does little to actually establish your expertise.

Anyone can call themselves a Business Expert. Have they been in business for many years? Have they successfully built and sold a company? Are they making a significant income? Do they know the inner workings of a specific type of business or industry?

Establishing expert status is, therefore, not only about your positioning and messaging, it's also, and more importantly, about doing the right things to be seen as an expert and build your credibility. I'll share four ways to establish your credibility in a moment.

First, let's look at how you can demonstrate your expertise.

Here are ten methods you can use—the more the better—to raise the market's awareness of you and be seen as an expert.

1) Write a book
2) Create a white paper
3) Put on webinars
4) Develop an educational video
5) Offer a free value-packed report
6) Speak to organizations
7) Publish articles in local print media
8) Write guest articles for other blogs
9) Get interviewed on the radio
10) Offer your services to a non-profit

Now, let's look at credibility.

In Larina Kase's book, *Clients, Clients, and More Clients,* she shares researcher B.J. Fogg's model on how people perceive credibility.

Here are the four key types:

- **Presumed** - This type of credibility is based on ideas and assumptions people hold.

- **Reputed** - This is based on other people's experiences and can be seen through testimonials, referrals, and endorsements.

- **Surface** - This is based on initial observation and first impressions and tends to be visual in nature.

- **Earned** - This is based on our own experiences with something or someone and develops over time.

Anyone who wants to become a successful consultant will find it worthwhile to give more thought to these four points.

Let's explore them in more detail.

Presumed Credibility

One way of achieving this kind of credibility is to write a book. Another is to work for a well-known company. As soon as prospective clients learn one of these facts about you, they are likely to presume you are an expert in your subject matter.

Reputed Credibility

As the above list shows, to achieve this kind of credibility, you want to amass as many testimonials as you can. Remember, there is a right way and a wrong way to get testimonials from clients. If you haven't been focusing on getting testimonials, referrals, and endorsements in your business, now is the time to start.

Surface Credibility

This is where image comes in and when first impressions matter most. Does your consulting website look professional? Are your business cards well designed? If you have clients to your office, are they getting the right impression? And how about the way you dress? Each one of these influences how people perceive you and judge you.

Earned Credibility

This type of credibility is your dividends. Where presumed, reputed, and surface credibility help you get in the door and close the initial sale, earned credibility can take a bit longer to develop. The main way you achieve this is by providing your clients with great results. Exceed their expectations. Deliver value. As you work with your client, you begin to earn more and more earned credibility.

Achieving credibility and expert status is a cycle. The more you push to be seen as an expert, the more you build your credibility and the more people view you as an expert. The cycle keeps growing and strengthens your authority as you continue these activities over time.

The second way to earn clients' trust is through the use of effective testimonials. Testimonials are one of the most powerful forms of proof you can offer prospective clients. Not only that, but the media enjoy them as well.

If you don't have any testimonials, stop right now, make a list of past or current clients, past employers or other professionals you've worked with. Then write them each a short email and ask if they could give you a testimonial.

Tip: When asking for testimonials, it's always best to provide a previous testimonial as a guide or, even better, write a draft testimonial to show them what kind of statement you are looking for. Let them know this is just an example, and they can alter it any way they want.

For example, you could send an email to your client, the president of a manufacturing company, and say:

"Hi, Tom,

Hope you're having a great week.

I'm updating some of my marketing materials and am in the process of collecting testimonials from clients and wanted to ask you for one.

I know you're very busy, so I put together a sample to save time:

'Mike really knows his stuff. He's helped our company generate five times more leads for less than we were spending before. He's reliable, professional, and a real pleasure to work with.'

Tom, would something like this be okay to use? Feel free to edit the sample and put it in your own words. Really, whatever works for you.

Thanks,

Michael"

Another Tip: Your testimonials should be as detailed as possible. Having a statement from someone that says, "James is really a great guy. He did great work," does very little to build credibility for you. It's too vague to represent real value. If that same testimonial read, "James really knows his stuff.

He helped our company transition smoothly from a recent merger, increased our productivity line by 10 percent in a month, and helped our sales team get back on track," that would be much more powerful.

Another way to build trust is simply by showing results. You can list your accomplishments and how you've helped others. Ideally, however, you should try to have testimonials from clients that talk about the results you've helped them achieve.

Good testimonials are detailed and clearly show how you are adding value, and why you're the real deal. They exude trust, make your offering more believable, and provide proof that you can generate results.

These kinds of testimonials help to cut right through many of the objections you may face from prospective clients when they're trying to decide if they will work with you.

4. Ask for Action

An ad or other marketing material that includes all of the above elements but neglects to include a proper call to action will see dramatically lower response rates.

At the end of all marketing material, after you have your Dream Client's attention, have made them promises and then proven how you can deliver, it's now time to ask them to take action. If you don't, they won't. If you do, they just may follow you.

Most business owners tend to overanalyze. If you fill them with information and leave them alone, they'll either keep spinning in a circle or quickly dismiss all the information and go on with their lives.

You don't want that to happen.

The only way around that is to ask them to take action. Request that they do something. That "something" could be to request a free report, watch a video on your website or blog, contact you for a complimentary evaluation or seminar. You need to clearly ask them to take the next step in the process.

Marketing Consulting By-Products

There is one other type of marking material that you should not overlook. In the creation and delivery of most products and services, by-products are produced. The majority of business owners and consultants pay little attention to these. They ignore them or don't even know they exist.

Identifying your consulting by-products and marketing them can bring a whole new stream of revenue for your business.

Take the consultant who gives presentations and seminars on a regular basis. She decides to compile all her notes and teachings to create a webinar that she charges for. That's a by-product. Creating videos or a book out of her notes and teachings would be another by-product. And a new stream of income is created.

Consulting Success

The web designer is busy creating websites for his clients. He finds himself creating many websites for lawyers. Rather than continuing with business as usual, he decides to launch a service of website templates designed specifically for law firms. It's a targeted and popular offering. It generates new revenue.

What by-products are you overlooking?

Pitfalls of Penny Pinching Your Marketing

Two consultants left their consulting firm at the same time to open their own businesses. One decided not to spend money on marketing. Instead, he chose the free route. He kept busy doing everything that he could to get his name out there.

The other consultant decided to spend $1,000 on some targeted marketing. He created his ideal list of clients, put together a campaign to go after them, and then proceeded to spend his money on reaching them.

The first consultant didn't spend any money. He got a lot done, but unfortunately, just getting things done isn't enough. Making money and landing consulting clients is what counts.

The second consultant spent $850 on his campaign and landed two clients. Each one worth over $15,000 to him. Not a bad return on investment (ROI).

Consulting Success

The self-employed (consultants, freelancers, independent professionals) are often a conservative bunch. They like to keep busy and do whatever they can to NOT spend money on their own marketing. Five dollars or $10 isn't a big deal, but as soon as you get over that magic threshold where the amount becomes something you have to think about, things change.

The human mind works in strange ways. It seems even if the ROI is sure to be greater than the cost, people still find it hard to pay.

Here is a good example. I was running an online marketing campaign for a client's firm in a very competitive industry. The results achieved had been nothing short of spectacular. We're talking about ROI of 6-to-1 or higher. That is, for every $1 they invested in the campaign, they generated $6 in revenue.

My recommendation to them was that it was time to increase the campaign budget. Why? Because if you know you're going to get back more than you're putting in, it makes sense to start scaling the campaign and driving more revenue.

But the company found it difficult to proceed. And they are not alone.

In many situations, companies and people have a hard time putting their money into something even when they know the potential to earn back many times their investment is great.

While this kind of thinking is understandable, it's also flawed. Why? Because it holds back the potential for greater success.

The saying, "It takes money to make money," isn't always true. Yet, it frequently is.

I don't advocate spending money on twenty different things in a shotgun approach to land clients. That's a waste. But spending money on your education, improving your skills, and on your own marketing in a targeted and direct way is often the best investment you can make.

Don't skimp. Invest in yourself.

The Consultants Marketing Budget

I sent a survey to the more than 29,000 consultants on our list, gathering insight about how much they spend on marketing, as well as what types of marketing they've found to be most effective. By discovering what has worked for others, you can adjust and hone your own marketing efforts.

What Type of Marketing Do You Spend the Most Time on?

Based on my research, it seems consultants tend to favor generating referrals and developing their network. These two marketing methods are known to be effective for any service professional, so this doesn't come as a surprise.

Many use social media and or educational marketing through writing and reports. Oddly, I've found that few consultants spend time on advertising their consulting business, even though advertising in a very targeted way can generate strong ROI. Opportunity exists here.

What Type of Marketing Makes Consultants the Most Money?

Which marketing strategies and tactics are making consultants the most money? That's the answer everyone wants to know.

Most consultants claim that referrals and networking generate the highest ROI. Presentations and seminars come in a distant second, followed by cold calling. I don't actually recommend cold calling. It's uncomfortable and awkward. Instead, I teach a process of connecting with ideal clients in a targeted way, building relationships with them, and then bringing calls into the mix later on, when it's effective.

Also, just because referrals and networking came in first on the survey, that doesn't mean they are the most effective approach for everyone. Their high rank largely comes from the fact that so many consultants are comfortable using these techniques.

I strongly recommend developing a marketing system in your business that doesn't rely on referrals, so you create a consistent pipeline of opportunities.

How Much Money Do Consultants Spend Marketing Their Business?

On average, I've found that most consultants spend about $7,500 marketing their businesses annually, though I've seen individual consultants spend as much as $200,000.

Consulting Success

On the other end of the spectrum, I know some consultants who spend nothing on marketing. Typically, this comes from being new to marketing, undervaluing its importance, or having a consulting business that is so well-established that they don't need to promote themselves.

Balancing Marketing Consulting Services with Client Work

M*any new consultants struggle to balance their time between delivering for a client engagement and business development for future work.*

I've read research that shows that most consultants spend 110 days every year working on their marketing and administration. These are days they are not doing client work. And while some people might offer a specific percentage to split the time, I'd suggest that every person and each business requires a different balance.

If you're working with just a client or two and really want to boost your work load and income, you'll want to increase the amount of time you spend on marketing your consulting services. When you're at the point that you have enough work to keep you busy for the foreseeable future, then you can reduce your marketing activities to as little as one day a week.

Consulting Success

What I suggest to my consulting clients and those getting started is to schedule a portion of every day or every other day for marketing activities. For example, if you want to land several new clients within six months, you could spend the first two hours of every day putting together your plan, implementing it, and taking action on it to achieve your goal.

However, make sure that not only are you spending sufficient time on marketing activities to land new clients, but that you are doing the right ones and doing them consistently.

Remember, there are only three ways to increase consulting sales. It doesn't matter what type of business you run or what kind of consulting you specialize in.

- You can increase the number of clients you work with.

- You can increase the size of the sale to each client.

- You can increase the number of times a client buys from you.

Many business owners and consultants I meet forget this timeless principle.

So, before you spend time trying to come up with that next magical marketing plan, or planning that big PR blitz, be sure to ask yourself if what you're doing is going to directly connect to one of the three ways to increase sales.

Some Words of Marketing Wisdom

You will increase your consulting sales if you are willing to put time into correct and consistent marketing activities. It will take some motivation to make this happen, and I have learned that sometimes motivation can come in the form of great words by great people. So, I would like to offer a series of great marketing and business quotes for you. Think about how you can incorporate this advice into your practice or draw on these words when things get challenging.

- *"Marketing's job is to convert societal needs into profitable opportunities."* – Anonymous

- *"If you believe in something, work nights and weekends, it won't feel like work."* – Kevin Rose

- *"You must either modify your dreams or magnify your skills."* – Jim Rohn

- *"We are really competing against ourselves, we have no control over how other people perform."* – Pete Cashmore

Consulting Success

- *"When you're ready to quit, you're closer than you think."* – Bob Parsons

- *"The only way around is through."* – Robert Frost

- *"Forget about your competitors, just focus on your customers."* – Jack Ma

- *"Whatever the mind of man can conceive and believe, it can achieve. Thoughts are things! And powerful things at that, when mixed with definiteness of purpose, and burning desire, can be translated into riches."* – Napoleon Hill

- *"Whatever you're thinking, think bigger."* – Tony Hsieh

- *"The entrepreneur always searches for change, responds to it, and exploits it as an opportunity."* – Peter F. Drucker

- *"When people are placed in positions slightly above what they expect, they are apt to excel."* – Richard Branson

- *"Long-range planning works best in the short term."* – Doug Evelyn

- *"Timing, perseverance, and ten years of trying will eventually make you look like an overnight success."* – Biz Stone

- *"Success in business requires training and discipline and hard work. But if you're not frightened by these things, the opportunities are just as great today as they ever were."* – David Rockefeller

- *"Always deliver more than expected."* – Larry Page

- *"The only limits are, as always, those of vision."* – James Broughton

- *"Vision is the art of seeing things invisible."* – Jonathan Swift

Consulting Success

- *"Any time is a good time to start a company."* – Ron Conway

- *"The golden rule for every business man is this: Put yourself in your customer's place."* – Orison Swett Marden

- *"The best way to predict the future is to invent it."* – Dennis Gabor

- *"The way to get started is to quit talking and begin doing."* – Walt Disney

Checklist: Marketing Your Consulting Services

☐ I've answered the six questions to see how prepared I am to market my consulting services.

☐ I have set my criteria to find my ideal, new clients.

☐ I have created a plan for my multi-step marketing campaign.

☐ I understand the two buying factors of clients.

☐ I have created an educational approach plan to establish myself as an authority.

☐ I understand the four areas each of my marketing materials should include.

☐ I have identified my possible marketing by-products.

☐ I understand the pitfalls of not investing money in my marketing strategies.

☐ I understand the three ways to increase consulting sales.

☐ I have read motivational quotes and will add those I find in my daily work to the list.

CHAPTER 9:
MANAGING CLIENTS AND RELATIONSHIPS

Clients and Relationships

A consultant's business is always a relationship business. Your level of success is directly connected to the level of service, satisfaction, and happiness you provide your clients. In short, they are the lifeblood of your business—never forget this.

Your Easiest Differentiator

One of the easiest and most effective ways to differentiate yourself from all the other consultants in your industry is by truly caring about your clients. Caring for your consulting clients is marketing. This isn't just a touchy-feely idea. It doesn't mean you're giving them a big hug every chance you get.

Caring means they know you care about them, their business, their interests, and their profits. It means you help and support them at every reasonable opportunity.

Caring is going out of your way for clients and doing something for them that others won't. Caring is listening to them rather than talking over them.

Caring is when you tell them something they may not want to hear or that might jeopardize your work, but it's in the best interest of their company.

Caring is tangible and is expressed by actions you take and the promises you make and keep.

Being Responsive

How many times have you left a message for someone or sent them an email, and they didn't respond for days? In fact, YOU are the one who has to follow up and get in touch with them.

I'll never forget working with one particular client a couple of years ago. They had worked with a design consulting firm to help with many of their marketing materials. I was brought on board to help them with their marketing and to increase revenue. During this process, I needed to update some design materials. I called the design consultant, he didn't pick up, so I left a message.

The next day I still hadn't heard back, so I sent him an email. Two days later, I got an email back saying he's quite busy and would get back to us in a couple of days. He didn't, and I had to follow up with him to get any action on his part. Here I was trying to bring him more business!

This might sound like a one-off story, but I've dealt with countless consultants, managers, and even executives who run their businesses this way.

There is nothing wrong with being so busy you can't take on more work. But, that's no reason for being unresponsive. Working this way makes you look unprofessional and tarnishes your brand and your name.

So many people seem to be well-intentioned, but when it comes to communication skills and professionalism, they offer what you might expect from an elementary school student. Rather than complain about this and ridicule such people, you're better off using it to your advantage.

You see, for every ten people that don't follow through, one will. And that one stands out. That one earns trust, respect, and becomes the someone people depend on.

Sometimes doing something that's bad for your business can actually turn out to be the best thing for it.

If you've ever emailed us here at ConsultingSuccess.com, you know that I answer almost every email myself—minus the spammers and the "we'll get you onto the first page of Google in five minutes" crapshooters. Most people would believe this approach doesn't make great business sense. It doesn't scale very well. And in some ways, they are right. It doesn't. But people sure do appreciate getting a reply from a real person within a reasonable amount of time. That's hours, not days.

"Thanks so much for getting back to me so quickly."

"You really have given great support!"

"Wow, I really appreciate the reply!"

We get messages like this from people all the time. People don't expect this level of service anymore, and that's a real shame. These days, it has become common place to email someone and not receive a reply for two or three days, sometimes a week or more. Sometimes you never get a reply. That's not very professional and no way to run a consulting business.

It might be hard work, it might take a lot more time, but it's a great way to build a sustainable business backed by customers who are happy to tell the world about you.

Consulting Success

My customers come from all over the world. They are expert consultants, long-time business owners, mid-level practitioners, and those just becoming consultants. Regardless of where they are from or what level of expertise they have, I do my best to respond as quickly as possible.

The result? First, people are shocked, excited, and delighted with the customer service I provide. Second, they trust me more because they know a real person will actually answer them. Third, it sets me apart from others who don't provide this level of service. And fourth, it's great for business.

That's right. Taking the time to respond in a professional manner is actually good for business. I hope that doesn't surprise you. If it does, that's okay. It means you have a great opportunity to improve on what you're currently doing.

I'm not sharing all of this with you to toot my own horn or to flood my inbox. My goal is that you look at your own communications and see if there are things that you can do to improve the level of care and service you provide to your own clients and customers.

I'm also putting this out there as a way for us to remain accountable as my business continues to grow, so that I ensure I'm continually providing a level of service that not only satisfies you, but delights you. It might be hard work, it might take a lot more time, but it's a great way to build a sustainable business backed by customers who are happy to tell the world about you.

Promise and Deliver

If you make a promise, keep it. If you've told a client that you'll get them the report they've asked for by Thursday, send it by Thursday, if not earlier.

Clients may not tell you this directly, but they judge everything you do. Even in their subconscious, their minds are forming opinions and feelings about the way you work.

If they don't fully trust you, respect you, and appreciate the work you are doing for them, when another consultant comes around and makes a bigger promise than you have or says they'll charge less, your client may be inclined to consider moving their business to someone else.

One of the easiest ways to keep your clients loyal is to meet and exceed their expectations.

You probably know how notoriously unreliable construction companies are when building residential houses. They typically tell you your house will be ready in May, but May comes and goes, and you don't get into your new house with all work done until July or August.

That has become the standard. People know to expect this. Similarly, business owners have come to expect that many consultants and employees aren't as professional as they'd like. They deal with it because they feel they have to; it's the only option.

Well, imagine their surprise and delight when you come along and provide them with responsive and caring service. You keep your promises, are on time for meetings, keep professional communications, and are pleasant to work with.

Consulting Success

It doesn't matter if you think you're providing good service. It doesn't matter if your website or brochure says that you do. All that matters is what your clients think.

Let me share with you a true story.

For the blog on my website, I was using a commenting system to manage all of the comments I receive. I decided on a service. Before my programmer installed it for me, I researched what the options were in the marketplace.

I narrowed it down to two. I sent both companies an email to get more information. The first company, and the one I chose, replied quickly with a full answer. The second took much longer to get back to me, and the reply was one sentence long—insufficient for a full response.

That was over two years ago. Things have changed.

When I redesigned the ConsultingSuccess.com blog, my commenting system started to act up. My programmer tried everything to fix it, but it was a no go. I sent one email to the system provider's support to get some help. No reply. Then I sent another. And a third.

I wasn't happy. Providing my readers with a great experience and way to comment and interact with the community on the blog is very important to us. So, I didn't take this whole thing lightly. I needed a solution.

And since I wasn't getting one from the provider, I decided to look at alternatives.

Finally, I got a response from the provider. It only took 72 hours! And the reply didn't help me solve the problem. So, I emailed them back…and again, I waited. But waiting wasn't an option. So, I switched over to the second company I had initially researched.

My new company has come a long way. Before switching to them, I sent them an email and they responded within 24 hours (it was probably more like 12 hours). The commenting system has everything I need, and so far, I'm very happy with it.

Why should you care about my commenting system troubles? Because, it's relevant for every consultant.

You NEED to provide the best service to your customers and delight them. If you fail to delight your customers at every turn, at some point their patience will end, and when it does, they will look for an alternative. They will find another consultant who can do what you can and that they believe can provide them with better service along the way.

If you're in an industry that doesn't have any competition, you're lucky. In that case, your client can't really jump ship. But these days, there are more options than ever before. The industry and product without competition is rare.

That's why you need to stay sharp. Always be on top of your game. And make it priority number one to keep your clients happy. If you don't, if for some reason you believe you're above that, or that everything is A-Okay, be prepared— you might be in for a rude awakening.

Meeting and exceeding your clients' expectations is crucial. Here are a few tips to meeting your clients' expectations.

- Be on time for every meeting. In fact, arrive five minutes early.

- Return phone calls and emails within hours or minutes, if you can and it doesn't interrupt your other work. It will blow your clients' minds.

- Do what you say you'll do. If you promise to follow up or provide more information—do it! Period.

- Deliver results. This is one is HUGE. Provide the results you and your client agreed to for the project or exceed them. This is the most powerful point.

- Send your clients gifts and notes of appreciation.

- Email your clients when you find a news report, study, or other bit of information that is relevant to their business, even if they didn't ask for it. Anything you can do to show your clients that you're thinking of them says a lot about you.

Do you see how just these simple things can make you stand out in the marketplace?

Small Things Add Up

S ome simple things you do, or don't do, can also make you stand out—in a bad way.

A big mistake many consultants and independent professionals make when first getting started in the consulting business is trying to act like they know it all.

If a client asks you a question and you don't know the answer, don't try to fudge it.

There's nothing wrong with not knowing everything. Your client won't look down on you if you don't have the specific answer they are looking for that moment. If you know the answer, that's great, but if you don't, what should you do?

The best course of action is to simply tell them, "I am not sure at the moment, but I will look into it, confirm the answer, and get back to you very soon."

The next step? Do it. As soon as your meeting is done, and you have a chance to find out the answer, you should email or call them with it. They will be impressed.

Often, your client will have already forgotten that they asked you for that information, so it shows your enthusiasm and follow-up skills. You end up coming across as very professional.

Customers notice when you choose not to go the extra mile. Don't take shortcuts. The problem with shortcuts is what you skip over. One shortcut on a project might not be a big deal, but a bunch of little ones add up—quality suffers, and it reflects poorly on you and your business.

I'll give you an example and share a piece of advice that has served me well over the years.

I was preparing for a monthly client strategy session and asked a contractor working for me to complete some research and put it all together so I could use it at the meeting.

When he finished the work and sent it over to me, I wasn't happy. While he had gathered some information and had done the research, it sat disorganized on the page and wasn't complete.

Little pieces of critical information were missing. A price here, a stat there. They made up maybe 15 percent of the content, but without them the document wasn't ready for the meeting.

It wouldn't have taken the contractor long to add this other information. In fact, he just needed to access the websites that he had already listed and spend a couple more minutes writing down a few more numbers.

Why didn't he do it? Because he was lazy and wanted to take the shortcut. It's not just him, though. The business world is filled with people who try to take shortcuts.

When you go to a meeting, you need to be overprepared.

Too many consultants go to meetings with the bare minimum. The problem is they know what they want to say, but they forget to take into account the questions their clients may ask them.

Being overprepared gives you confidence. You walk into that meeting with everything in order, and no matter what question your client springs on you, more times than not, you're prepared to answer them and have documents to show them.

Don't Get Complacent

I'd been with the same dentist for at least ten years. He's friendly, personal, generally punctual, and knows his way around the mouth. He does what I expect a dentist to do, and he does it quite well. For that reason, I'd never thought about changing dentists.

Then, one day, my dentist moved to a new office. A larger one. And now there are three dentists all working under the same roof. The staff is friendly. The design of the new office is great. It even has the latest technology with flat screen TVs, remote controls, computers.

Luckily, not too much had changed. But something was about to.

I called to change the date of my next appointment, as I was going overseas. My dentist was unavailable, but one of the other dentists in the office was. Sure, I'd give him a try, I thought. That next appointment changed everything.

This new dentist was younger, albeit less experienced, but it didn't seem that way. He was much more personal, asked important questions, spent more time with me, and did a more thorough job.

That experience opened my eyes to the quality I was missing from my current dentist. I had come to expect quality and service that was good. But the new dentist provided something great. Now, every time I book an appointment, I ask for the new dentist. He's won my business.

The lesson: Don't become complacent. Don't accept standard, average, or just good enough, because the day someone provides better results, service, or quality than you is the day your client's loyalty will dry up. Left unchecked and uncorrected, so, too, may your business.

Make Your Opinion Heard

Another mistake many consultants make is not making their opinion heard. At first glance, not expressing your opinion even when it goes against what your client wants may not seem like a big problem.

They're paying you; your job is to keep them happy, right? Wrong!

Of course, you need to keep your client happy. However, most people who find themselves in this situation fail to recognize that their clients actually WANT to be proved wrong from time to time.

They are paying you for your professional opinion, not to simply agree with them all the time. The fear that you'll get axed for "going against the boss" rarely becomes a reality. It's understandable that many people have trouble crossing the brass by telling them they are wrong. Most business owners tend to have strong opinions, and they are not always the most approachable people.

That must not stop you.

Your job, as difficult as it seems, is to always tell your client your true opinion, not what you think they want to hear, even if it goes against what they believe is right.

To clarify. This doesn't mean you go around telling your clients they are wrong and leave it at that. When you counter with a different opinion, you'd better have a reason or case study you can use to explain your reasoning.

What you'll find is that your client will appreciate what you have to say. And while they may not at first, if you have some proof or a strong reason as to why your proposal is correct, there's good chance they'll go with your recommendation.

Even if they don't, no worries. At the end of the day, it's not about a stirring up a coup. It's about making sure that your opinion is known and that you do what you can to support your case—in your client's best interest.

If they choose to disregard your opinion, and things don't turn out the way they should have, at least they know your position, and they can't come back and blame you.

Time Is Money

Time is money. This is true for both you and your client. Most business owners appreciate you getting to the point and respecting their time and resources. Meetings are big places where you can show your respect for your client by keeping them moving.

When meetings go off course, your time is being wasted. Projects receive less attention than they deserve. Here are five things to keep in mind, so you can turn meeting chatter into focused and productive client interactions.

1. Small Talk

Small talk is necessary in many situations. For example, if you are just starting to build your relationship with a new client or prospect, it's fine and normal to talk about the weather, sports, news, and so on to warm things up. In fact, this can be a very important part of strengthening your relationship with your client.

2. Keep It Under Control

Once you've developed a strong working relationship with your client, you should start to guide every meeting to business matters as quickly as possible. If the purpose of the meeting isn't to get to know each other, then stop gnawing at the bone and get to the meat.

3. The Value of Focus

Remember, clients hire you because of your expertise and what you can do for them. They know you need to actually do work to get things done. By showing them that you want to spend your time with them focused on the business, it demonstrates your desire to get them results.

4. Give Direction

Just because your client is paying you doesn't mean they should be the boss. They, too, need direction. If you allowed your client to do everything their way…well, they wouldn't be any farther ahead and wouldn't need you, would they?

As I talked about in a previous post on "Making Your Opinion as a Consultant Count," it's okay to go against what your client wants—in fact, they respect that. If the meeting is floating around, especially if there are several people in the room, it's your job to make your voice heard (in a polite way), and get the meeting back on track.

5. Straight and Friendly

To get the attention of the people you're meeting with, wait for a break in the conversation and prepare to make your move. As soon as one person finishes their sentence, dive in and use one of these:

- *"Okay guys, let's get back to..."*

- *"We should probably move on to..."*

- Hold up a piece of paper with your notes and say, *"Next we should talk about..."*

- *"Sorry guys, but I only have until 2 pm today, so it would be great if we can..."*

I'd avoid saying things like this (unless you're very close with your clients):

- *"Yo! We need to get back to..."*

- *"Hey! Lets' focus on..."*

You get the idea. If you think it's better to stay quiet and let your client run the show, think again. That would be a mistake.

That said...

Extra Point: It's Case by Case

Sometimes you just need to listen. I remember sitting down with a client and feeling more like her therapist than her consultant and advisor. She had a lot going on in her life, and it was affecting her business as well. I could tell she needed to vent.

In that case, my job wasn't to push for business talk but rather to listen to her and support her, so she could refocus herself, feel better, and as a result, her business would benefit.

Keeping Your Clients on Your Side

Nothing keeps your clients happier than you doing good work and producing results. Even if you're a pain to work with, if you can really deliver, they'll be inclined to stick with you. They'll probably talk behind your back and call you a pain in the neck, but if you're delivering, they'll keep you on their side.

That's not to say that you should aim for this. Yes, work hard and ensure you are delivering results, but keep them happy. This includes showing them how important they are to you. A great way to keep them on your side is by sending gifts and notes of appreciation.

Too many consultants spend little to no money on demonstrations of appreciation to their clients. This isn't about buying their business; it's about building and strengthening the relationship.

How much money should you be spending on your clients each year?

If you're getting paid even just $1,000 a month from a client, that's $12,000 a year. Would it be reasonable for you to spend $200 to $400 a year showing them that you appreciate their business?

When I've enjoyed a great bottle of wine, I'll often go back to the store and grab a few more bottles, bring them back to the office, attach a card to each, and have them delivered to my clients. In such cases, I don't say, "Thank you for your business," as that sounds like you're trying to buy their happiness.

Instead, I write a short note that says something like, "Mark, I enjoyed this great bottle of wine last night and thought you might, too. Regards, Michael." That's it. Their first thought when they get it is, "Wow, that's nice of him." And that's my goal. They think it's nice, and they appreciate knowing that I appreciate them. That's part of building the relationship.

Little things like that throughout the year are great ways to differentiate yourself from others in the market and to continue receiving your clients' business.

A couple of times a year, I also send a gift basket - one with some tropical fruit and another with chocolates.

Reward the Best

Who are your best consulting clients? It probably won't take you very long to figure out who they are. When I say best, I don't mean the friendliest or nicest or even your favorite clients.

By best, I mean your most loyal and valuable.

The ones that have been with you the longest and spend the most money with you.

You probably know exactly who they are. How are you treating them? The same as all your other clients? Maybe you believe all clients should be treated equally?

Well, if your best clients are getting lumped in with all your other clients, it's time to make some changes.

Your best clients should be treated differently. Why? Because it only makes sense to spend more time, energy, and money to keep the people who are paying you the most as happy as can be.

What does treating them better look like? It can include things like:

- Responding to their emails and calls more quickly.

- Making more room in your schedule to see them at their convenience.

- Going the extra mile for them, not just once or twice, but every time.

- Offering to help them in any way you can anytime the opportunity arises.

- Sending them gifts and notes of appreciation, not only on the major holidays but also at unexpected times.

- Referring them additional business.

- Constantly looking for new opportunities to help them grow their business.

Consulting Success

Keeping your best clients happy will help them to stay your best clients.

That's not only good sense, it's good business.

Dealing with Client Problems

Most problems with clients arise from miscommunication. The most likely culprit is email. Our reliance on this tool has led to the deterioration of our communication skills.

It's not that I dislike email. I use it heavily each day, but there are some people who seem afraid to pick up the phone and talk with their clients. So, they always send emails. That's a big mistake.

Here's an example that illustrates the challenges of email. When you try to set a meeting by email, how many back-and-forth messages does it usually require? One to make the suggestion, another one to say, "Yeah that's a good idea, but how about one day later," then a response saying, "Great, and let's do it at 10 am," and then a final one saying, "Great, see you then."

You're looking at an average of four to five emails to set a meeting. Compare this to picking up the phone and making that meeting. One call, done.

Consulting Success

The worst example of this is when you receive an email from a client who seems unhappy. The novice consultant will reply to that email with another email that tries to solve the problem. Unfortunately, that rarely works. The experienced consultant will pick up the phone and call the client. They'll review together what the issue is and discuss some possible solutions. Nine times out of ten, this works extremely well.

It's really no one's fault. Email lacks a great deal of information we use to solve problems.

If you ever get an unhappy-looking email from a client, here are two suggestions:

1) Email them right back and set up a time to meet in person. This is the ideal situation for more complex problems.

2) Pick up the phone right away and call the client. Talking on the phone provides so much more information that in almost all cases, you'll be able to resolve the issue right then and there.

Email is a great tool, but its curse is that it leads people to make a great deal of assumptions. This doesn't have to be the case, nor should it.

When and How to Fire Your Clients

I've been fortunate enough not to have to deal with this situation very often. In all the years I've been a consultant, while I've turned down numerous projects, I've only had to let go of two clients. "Fire" is such a strong word, but it's the way most of us think about it.

None of us like to do this, it's counter-intuitive, but the fact is, sometimes it has to be done.

So first, let's talk about why you should even consider letting a client go, and then we'll dig into how to do it.

Getting Sleepy

If you're not learning anything new and not enjoying the project, it's time to look at making a change. Your level of interest and passion shows through your work, so either get into it or get out. If you're in the financial position to pick and choose your work, then you shouldn't be spending your time on projects that you're not having fun with. This doesn't mean every minute is going to be a party, but you should be stimulated and constantly learning.

They Just Don't Care

If your client is always slow to respond, tough to get a meeting with, and shows little interest in the project, it's a sign that they may not value the work you are doing or just don't care. That's not the kind of client relationship you want. You'll save yourself a lot of hassle and stress, because this is the kind of client you are going to have to chase to get answers from.

Show Me the Money

If you're putting in tons of work and not getting compensated fairly, do something about it. Either tell the client you need to bill for additional hours or that you need to increase your consulting fees. If they won't have any of that, it's time to head for the door. If you're doing a good job, you deserve to make money from the project.

No Action, No Results

A problem with some clients is that they take no action. They'll pay you, they may even tell you they are happy with your work, but when it comes time for them to implement your recommendations, nothing happens. This isn't so much a case of having to let them go as sitting down with them to figure out how you can help them to implement.

After all, if you work your behind off and the client doesn't follow-through, you won't see any results. And that comes back to bite you later on.

It's not easy to end a client relationship, but you only have so much time in each day, and it's just not worth spending that time working with people you don't enjoy working with.

Here's how you end it. First, set up a face-to-face meeting with your client and go over your concerns. Email doesn't work in this situation. Sitting down or talking on the phone is critical. Face-to-face is ideal (but not required). Show your client that you are genuinely concerned; tell them why and how they can turn things around.

If they seem to be agreeing with you and understand what needs to be done to make this a successful relationship, give it another go. If the client still seems withdrawn or passive, let them know that you want to continue working together, but if things continue the way they are, you won't be able to.

How to Say It

Word this in a way that puts the decision-making power into your client's hands—at least that is what they will feel. That way if they don't live up to their side of the bargain, it's easy for you to make an exit. You don't want to come across as being too strong and giving them the impression that "it's my way or the highway."

In most cases, you'll be able to turn things around. But if your client is causing you more stress than good, even if it's making you money, it's often not worth it. Once you end that troubled relationship, you'll feel relieved.

Plus, you'll then be free to find new clients that you enjoy working with more, and add new project income—all in short order.

The Power of Progress Reports

Progress reports are one of the most powerful ways to keep your clients happy, make sure the project is on track, and keep the work coming.

Most consultants are well-intentioned and have a plan to provide regular progress reports, but they don't.

A progress report is a simple (often one page) document that outlines three things:

1) What work has been completed and the results of that work.

2) What you are currently working on and its status.

What you'll be working on next (or suggest that you do) and the value it provides.

This three-step process sounds very simple, and it is. But the effect it has is quite deep and powerful. Let's dig into each of the three parts of the progress report:

Part 1 – When you tell your client what you've completed and show them the results, they feel good because it justifies spending their money and shows they made a good decision hiring you. Of course, if the results aren't good, you need to have a plan to explain why and how they'll be fixed.

Part 2 – By showing them what you are currently working on and giving them a status update on it, they can see that you are working hard, and again, it justifies continuing to pay you for your expertise.

Part 3 – This is a big one. By showing what the next steps are, or giving recommendations for the next steps, you're setting your clients up to understand and see the value of ongoing work.

If you don't have any next steps planned, figure some out that provide value to your client. It could be continued work on the same area of their business or work on a new area.

If you just focus on what you've agreed to do and don't work on lining up your next step, your project will come to a swift end, and you'll be leaving a great deal of money on the table.

Progress reports are extremely easy to put together. They can be as simple as a few sections on a piece of paper with bullet points, or a chart displaying results, or both.

This is an often-overlooked area of the consultant's role. But it's something you should definitely be doing on a regular basis.

Since most of my clients are set up as monthly retainer work, I provide them with progress reports on a monthly basis.

However, since these reports only take a short time to put together, I can whip one up at any time as needed.

The 10-Minute Income Increase Challenge

I am a big believer in strengthening relationships with clients, and the advice I have offered will increase your income. However, I want to demonstrate to you just how powerful managing your relationships with your clients really is and how fast it can make you money. Here's your challenge, if you choose to accept it.

In a minute, I'm going to give you the details of this challenge.

By now, you realize I'm a big believer in building and strengthening relationships with clients. When done the right way, it can turn a small project into a large one, a one-time payday into recurring annual income.

But now, let's get back to how you can make more money in the next ten minutes.

Here's what you need to do:

This involves contacting at least one consulting client, if not more. There are two approaches to this:

a) Think about the work you're currently doing for your client. Now think of what other services or products they would benefit from. What would be another way you can help them reach their goal?

b) Take five minutes and research their industry. Look for their competitors. Search their name. See what the latest news is. The key is finding information that is relevant to your client.

Your next step is to pick up the phone (the best way) or email your client. Tell them about your idea that would help their business, or the relevant news clipping or information you've found that "you thought they'd be interested in seeing."

That's it. Two simple steps

Why does this work?

This works and will make you more money because clients are always open to new ideas that will help THEM make more money. If you can think of something that will, they will want to hear about it.

Also, when you provide your clients with relevant information, it automatically says to them that you really are on their side, that you're going beyond just "doing your work." They must really be important if you're "just doing additional research on their company." They don't need to know it took you five minutes. It shows you care, and that translates into them wanting to continue working with you.

Do it right now! Don't put it off for a couple of hours or days. If you really want to make more money and be more successful, then put the excuses aside and make this happen this very moment.

You have the ability to add new profit to your business in 10-minutes—right now. We've put together a simple 10-Minute Income Increase Checklist so you can put this rain-making tactic into action.

Save a copy of our checklist and use these steps to help you generate quick revenue at consultingsuccess.com/bookbonus

Checklist: Clients and Relationships

☐ My clients consider me responsive to their needs.

☐ I deliver on all the promises I make to my clients.

☐ Last year I spent $_____ on my clients, this year I will spend $_____.

☐ I have identified those clients that are my best.

☐ If I ever have a problem with a client, I will call them or arrange a face-to-face meeting instead of relying on email.

☐ As much as possible, I will only work with clients I enjoy working with.

☐ I use (or will use) progress reports on a regular basis with my clients.

☐ I have taken the 10-Minute Income Increase Challenge.

CHAPTER 10:
CONSULTING SYSTEMS AND BILLING

Successful Consultants Use Systems

I've had the pleasure of not only working as a consultant for over a decade but also consulting and working with other consulting firms.

Between my own business and these consulting clients, I've had the opportunity to work in over twenty industries and get a first-hand look at how different consultants run their businesses.

Successful consultants use systems. They've either developed their own, or they've paid to take courses and learn from others, then adapted what they've learned to their businesses.

A system consists of processes, defined steps, and actions you or your client takes at each point along the way. An effective system is like a map. It shows you which way to go, but it also anticipates what you'll find around each turn and gives you options and ideas of how to proceed.

Creating Your Own

When you're new to consulting, it's a good idea to try your hand at developing your own system. The reason this is valuable is because it gives you the opportunity to work your way through your business and better understand what it is you really offer your clients and how you can best help them.

Systems Can Be Simple

Your system doesn't have to be complicated or elaborate. It doesn't have to be 100 pages with charts, diagrams, and formulas. It can be, but it doesn't have to be.

The core pieces of the best systems I've seen can often be condensed into a couple of pages, with simple documents to support each of the core areas. Let's look at how you can create your own system.

Getting Your System Going

To start creating your business system, take a good look at every activity you'll be involved in. List every action that you take from start to finish on your projects. You'll then find ways to document each step briefly.

For example, you might cover the following: From meeting with clients, to communicating with them, to sending them a proposal and contract, to helping them with the actual work you provide, and then billing them to get your money.

Each of the above steps should be part of your system. Let's break each down to clarify how this works:

Consulting Success

1) **Meeting with clients** – Create a short document that contains all of the main questions you ask clients when you meet with them for the first time. You can also include some points that you cover each time.

2) **Communicating with clients** – Are you sending emails, faxes, letters in the mail? For each one of these, you should have a proper template that includes all the information you need, along with your contact information and logo. That way you just update the current required content each time and send it out, streamlining your business.

3) **Proposal and contract** – You'll create a template for these. Each time you send it out, you just make the necessary adjustments. Instead of spending hours or days getting this ready, you can make the adjustments to the template and get it back to the prospective client in a couple of hours, so they don't cool down and will continue to think about how interested they are in working together. Speed and efficiency matter.

4) **Working documents** – This is the core of your system. Depending on what kind of consultant you are and what you want to accomplish with your clients, your documents will differ. However, the goal of all core documents is to take the knowledge and skill in your head and get it onto a piece of paper (or into a PowerPoint or Word file). This is where you'll likely create a process map that shows the steps and stages you take your client through in the project.

You'll have a sheet with effective questions that you can ask that will get the answers you need quickly, thereby allowing you to make better recommendations to your clients. You may also create a checklist that lists all the necessary or key areas or most common problems, and then use that to help your clients.

5) **Billing** – You've got to get paid, right? This part of your system should include your invoice, a receipt, and an Excel file or other software that allows you to track your time spent on projects.

Having these kinds of documents created, organized, and part of your system is what separates those who want to reach success but will have a very hard time making it from those who are well on their way to making it.

Your system will save you time, it will keep you more organized, and it will ensure that you stay on course and don't overlook anything. All of this means better results for your clients, which equals happier clients. Not to mention that you'll look far more professional showing up with a system, rather than a blank pad of paper.

Software Programs You Can Use to Streamline Your Business

There are also several online applications you can use to streamline your business. These are reasonably priced and will centralize all of your billing and related information in one place.

Freshbooks – (http://www.freshbooks.com/) This online application allows you to track the time you spend on projects, and helps to manage the billing and invoicing of your clients.

Quickbooks – (http://www.quickbooks.com/) Similar to Simply Accounting this is a full accounting system that lets you track your revenue and expenses. What's nice about a program like this is that you can also instantly create invoices for your clients. And at the end of the year, you simply send your accountant all the information or print it out for them.

Xero – (http://www.xero.com) Well-established accounting program that offers worldwide support.

Wave Accounting –(http://www.waveaccounting.com) Wave Accounting is currently free and provides all the bells and whistles you'd want in a standard accounting program. It is also hosted in the cloud like Xero and Freshbooks.

Harvest – (http://www.getharvest.com) A well-designed time-tracking application that will help you keep track of the time you spend on projects and ensure you spend your time productively.

Evernote – (http://www.evernote.com) This website and mobile app allow you to store and organize all kinds of information, from audio files and voice recordings, to photos, videos, text files, web clippings and more. You can create folders for each of your projects and keep relevant information in each, plus it is accessible from anywhere.

Basecamp – (http://www.basecamp.com) The leading online project management and collaboration tool. Basecamp allows you to manage all your projects more effectively. You can even share and discuss projects with your clients right within the application.

Infusionsoft – (http://www.infusionsoft.com) This is an all-in-one CRM, Marketing, and E-Commerce platform. It's not cheap, but it does save considerable time and makes your marketing more effective than piecing several different solutions together.

Ontraport – (http://ontraport.com) Ontraport is a direct competitor to Infusionsoft. Take a look at both products before making a decision, as some people like one over the other.

Hubspot CRM – (www.hubspot.com/CRM) Hubspot CRM provides up-to-the-minute tracking of all customer interactions with a clean, visual dashboard. Plus, it's completely free of charge, and there's no contract, credit card, or training required.

How to Get Paid on Time

You've had your client sign the agreement/contract that you put together. The project got off to a great start, everything seems fine and you send in your invoice to get paid.

Sounds okay, right? Well, you've just committed a consulting sin.

Yes, there will be some clients, like people you already know well or government projects, where you'll request payment only at the end of the month or when the project is complete. But for the most part, this isn't recommended.

After working so hard, you really shouldn't put yourself in the position to possibly not receive payment. Doing this in most situations will be fine, and you will get paid on time. However, it's not the only option, and certainly isn't the best one.

How can you ensure you'll get paid on time? Easy. Get paid before you start working. I request payment at the end of the current month or beginning of the next for my work to be done that next month. So if I'm starting to work in March, I'll ask for payment at the end of February or the first couple of days of March.

Do I give my clients 30 days to pay me? No, I ask them to pay within seven days. I'm not some large multinational that can or wants to wait a month to get paid. If I've busted my butt to get my clients results, there is no reason they shouldn't pay me promptly.

If you're dealing with a client who doesn't have enough money to pay you in such a manner, be careful—the day when they can't, won't, and don't pay you is just around the corner.

To some of you this may sound unreasonable. That's fine. There is no right or wrong. It always comes down to your relationship with the client and the situation you're in. However, most consultants spend a great deal of time wondering when they'll get paid. It's unfortunate because if you set yourself up for such a situation, you're worrying yourself unnecessarily.

From the start when you speak with your clients, let them know this is how you work, and this is how you get paid. If you do so early on and explain it without hesitation, it's unlikely you'll face any resistance.

Consultants need to deliver for their clients and go out of their way to make sure their clients are happy. The flip side of that is that clients are choosing to work with a consultant because they trust them and believe them to be an expert.

Once that relationship is in place, and it usually is when your client is a solid company, then your client should have no problem paying you in advance.

Whether they pay you for your whole month in advance, 50 percent, 33 percent, or 25 percent, it doesn't matter. What matters is that you've received payment for the work you are going to provide. If you're providing results and doing what you've agreed that you'll do, the client should have no issue complying with the billing cycle you set up for them. The exception might be if you're working with a large corporate client. Their procurement or HR department may have a specific billing schedule.

When you start working with a client, simply lay out the billing terms that you use. For example, payment for the month at the beginning of each month. And payment should be made within seven days of sending the invoice.

What should you do if you have an ongoing client who pays you after you've completed the work? If the relationship is going well and they always pay on time, you're more likely than not to continue receiving your checks right after your project is finished.

However, to change an existing client over, simply let them know that your company is using a new billing system to keep more organized and that all your clients are now paying you in advance or a certain percentage up front.

Again, if you're doing great work, you'll face very little resistance.

I've been doing this for many years, and I've rarely encountered a problem. We'll talk about what to do if you do face a problem next.

What to Do if Your Client Doesn't Pay on Time

If your client doesn't pay on time, the first thing you need to do is relax. Most of them will still pay you. They've either forgotten, are too busy, or are feeling a bit cash-strapped right now, and they just need a bit longer to get you your money.

If it's a small project, chasing a client endlessly and pushing them to get your money is about all you can do. If you're thinking of continuing to work with this client, then you don't want to come across as overly annoying. If you do, they may still not pay you and the relationship will be over.

In most cases, it's best to send a quick email or call to make sure they received your invoice as you haven't received payment yet. If you don't get a satisfactory answer or still haven't received your payment within a reasonable amount of time, the next step is to meet face to face with the client. Usually, meeting in person is the easiest way to discuss issues that are hard to talk about.

If it's a much larger project and you need to collect your money, and all other communications between you and the client fail, you can always bring in a collection agency. I've never had to do this, and I doubt I ever will, but that's because I don't set up my business to allow for non-payment.

This goes back to the previous section. If you structure your billing cycle properly and ask your client to pay you in advance, or even pay you certain portions throughout the project when you hit certain milestones, then you won't end up in this kind of situation.

Client problems like this one are almost always connected to a lack of communication, both on your part and on the client's part. Be clear about all of this from the start, set the expectations, and create a structure that leaves the least room for issues like this to occur. It's the best way to go; it's the right way to do it.

The Value of Outsourcing

As soon as you start getting some consulting income, you should look at outsourcing some of your more mundane tasks. Many consultants have trouble delegating tasks and feel that it makes more sense for them to do it all themselves.

I can tell you from experience, this is rarely the case. If you're billing a client approximately $100/hour or even $60/hour, doesn't it make sense to pay someone else $10 to $20/hour to do less essential tasks for you?

This will free up your time to work with more clients, spend more time on actual client work, or even allow you to take more time off.

The kinds of tasks you can easily outsource include transcriptions of audio or video interviews, video editing, website design, programming and other graphic design. You can even outsource the job an assistant would do for you, and they can prepare standard documents, set your meetings, and remind you of appointments.

Consulting Success

When should you do this? Ask yourself if the task you are doing is worth whatever your rate is? If it's nowhere near that, look to outsource it. Obviously, if it involves confidential information, like billing or client emails, you shouldn't be in a rush to outsource those. But for most straightforward tasks, try to get someone else to do it.

For example, I was working on a project and needed to collect a lot of data from a couple of websites. Next, the data needed to be entered into a spreadsheet so I could have it organized and analyzed. After analyzing the data, I needed to send out emails to hundreds of companies to make initial contact with them.

The data collection and entry took about four hours. The emailing of the data took another three hours. That would have been seven hours out of my day, or over a couple of days, that I'd have to spend on this work.

By no means do I find this kind of work enjoyable. So, I didn't do it, but I still got it done at a fraction of what it would have cost me to do it by outsourcing.

Outsourcing can do wonders for your business, and it's very easy to try. Several services like Elance.com and Odesk.com offer safe and easy ways for you to find people to outsource work to, track their hours, and make payments. You can see the level of experience each person has, feedback about them from other buyers, and what they charge.

You can always negotiate specific rates and a setup that would be most suitable to you. Until the day you want to hire another employee to join you (if you ever do), outsourcing is a great way to build your business.

Anytime I've outsourced a sizeable project on the cheap, it's been a flop. Communication is always the issue, and I find that the more details the project has, the more important it is to work with quality professionals who can communicate very clearly.

I've worked with people from Poland, Russia, the Philippines, India, Pakistan and other countries. It's not a specific country that's the problem. It's the detail and complexity of the project that requires a high level of communication. And because of that, outsourcing to people who can't communicate at a superior level often leads to disaster.

Stick with outsourcing straightforward and simple tasks, and you'll see how empowering it feels to get more work done, free up your time, and stay focused on the work that really counts the most.

Are you spending too much valuable time on low-level tasks? Our Quick-Start Guide to Hiring Your First Freelancer will help you identify your most important tasks. And you'll learn how to hire a freelancer to do the rest.

Build a more efficient, profitable consulting business where you can focus on high-level work by using our guide at consultingsuccess.com/bookbonus

Checklist: Billing and Systems

☐ I have outlined all of the areas in my business that I can create a system for.

☐ I have created materials that cover at least the five main parts of my consulting system as included in the chapter.

☐ I make it easy for my clients to understand that I need to get paid on time.

☐ I can outsource the following areas of my business: _____, _____, _____ and _____.

CHAPTER 11:
PRODUCTIVITY AND GROWTH

Success Demands Productivity

Productivity is a trait of successful consultants. Every professional wants to be more productive. The more productive you are the more you get done, the more money you make, and the more time off you can enjoy. You can put together the greatest marketing and client building strategy in the business, but it won't do any good if you aren't productive.

There are many ways to maximize your productivity. This includes creating a strategic plan, setting goals, managing your time, and watching out for common time wasters.

Creating a Strategic Plan for Consultants

I have often thought that there are many people who don't know what the word "strategy" really means.

Of all the consultants, freelancers, and business owners that I've spoken with over the years, few really understood the meaning of the word, and even fewer were putting it into practice the right way.

To many, having a strategy is about having an overly complicated plan to grow their business, a list, or several steps they need to take to achieve their goal.

Frankly, as an idea, that approach makes complete sense. However, the problem is most plans miss a critical check to see whether or not they are actually strategic.

The firm Strategos says to have a real strategy it must, first, "really matter to your existing and potential customers; and second, it differentiates you from your competition."

Now, let's dig a bit deeper into both of these points:

1. Matter to your existing and potential customers.

a) If your strategy and plans don't offer the value your customers are looking for, there really is no point. If someone needs chopsticks for their business and you're trying to sell them a better kind of fork, you're wasting your time.

b) Make sure that your focus and offer are what your market wants and that it really matters to them.

c) If it doesn't, you'll need to refocus on a different market where you can sell your offering, or go back to the drawing board, or modify your current offering for a better fit.

d) How will you know? The best way to find out what matters to your customers is to ask them. Ask as many customers or potential customers as you can, and then try to make the sale. In business, talk is cheap, money speaks, and you want to see people give you their hard-earned cash for what you're selling—that's the ultimate validation.

2. Differentiates you from the competition.

This one sounds simple, but it can be quite hard.

a) You may think what you're doing is unique. But if it's not, you'll have a hard time convincing the market to buy from you.

b) While searching online and doing research from your home or office is a great way to get an initial look to see if what you're offering is unique, it's just a start.

c) The best way to find out whether or not you have a real unique advantage over your competitors is to get out into the market and speak with the people who know the market better than you do.

d) A potential client will tell you quickly if what you're showing them or saying to them sounds the same as another firm.

e) And you'll know when you have a real differentiation strategy, because the people you talk to will say things like, "Wow, that's really great," and, "I've been wishing someone would do that."

So, before you do anything else, take a good look at your current strategy and business plans.

One Goal A Day Strategy

There are a ton of books out there that will teach you all kinds of techniques and approaches you can take to be more productive and better manage your time. For a consultant, especially one that works independently, staying on top, on the ball, and getting things done is key to success.

Yet even with so much literature on productivity, I continue to meet business owners and consultants who can't seem to stay productive. They may have bursts of activity, but like a kid jacked up on candy and soda pop, their activity flatlines rather quickly.

Is there hope for these people? I believe so.

A common problem is that the more productive you try to be, the less you'll actually achieve. People who have trouble being productive are usually trying to do too much.

Here's what happens. You may be naturally unorganized. You have real trouble getting into a system and working through it on a regular basis, but there's pressure all around you (most often coming from your own head).

Expectations are set, and now you feel like you have to do more and keep busy.

So, you throw more things on your plate, but they are little things, not ones that actually move your business forward. You trick your mind into believing you are getting things done. And then your mind shuts down. It's overloaded with all these to-dos you've scheduled for yourself.

The best approach I've seen is what I call the "One Goal a Day Strategy."

It is what it sounds like.

Set one goal for yourself each day. Now, before you get all excited thinking that you just need to do one thing and can then put your feet up for the rest of the day, let me be clear.

This goal needs to be important, something that actually moves your business forward. It can be writing an article and submitting it to a publication, getting a press release out, writing and sending out a promotion for your services, and so on.

Timing Is Key

The best time of day to do this work is early in the morning, before your brain goes into overdrive and gets stressed from everything else going on in your life. Before the phone starts ringing. Achieve your goal as quickly as possible and early in the day.

Consulting Success

It feels great to get something important done each day, and then you have the rest of the day to work on other aspects of your business. And when things do come up, as they always do, you'll have already done the most critical thing that you needed to do for your business that day.

You don't have to do 100 things a day to be productive. Start off by just focusing on one. Get it done. No excuses. No procrastination. Get it done early; get it out of the way. You'll feel great. Your confidence will grow. You'll get more done, and you'll find yourself becoming more productive as time goes on—not to mention all the good it will do for your business.

Other Proven Tactics to Increase Your Productivity

A search on Amazon.com for books on productivity returns 45,960 titles. If you're having trouble being productive at work, you may find it difficult to make the time to read a book on productivity cover to cover.

For that reason, I'm going to share with you five proven tactics that you can start implementing today that will enable you to increase your productivity and help you to get more done.

1) **Wake up early.** The morning provides a calm that is often hard to find at any other time of day. Phones aren't ringing, emails are only starting to trickle in. This is your time to get ahead. Use this time to exercise, read or study, and to get a jumpstart on your most important task of the day.

2) **Start with important work.** Our most meaningful and impactful projects are often the hardest and require the most time and attention. That's why they often end up getting pushed farther and farther on our to-do list throughout the day.

Take a new approach and start your day by focusing on your most important work first. You may find it hard to get going, but once you do, you'll be working on tasks that have meaning and provide a real impact to your business and career. Plus, once you get through your most important item, you'll feel liberated and can move on to the less important work that so often clogs the day.

3) **No interruptions.** Robin Sharma points to research data that says workers are interrupted every 11 minutes. Every distraction reduces your productivity and derails your focus and energy from the task at hand. Value your work and value your time by saying NO to interruptions. Close your door, create a "Do Not Disturb" sign if you need one and block your calendar with work times so your assistant or coworkers know not to bother you. There are so many interruptions around us each day. Find what they are in your life and start removing them.

4) **Avoid meetings.** Daily and weekly meetings can be critical to keep the flow and rhythm in a business, but meetings where several people need to spend twenty minutes to an hour or more need to be avoided like the plague. Not only do these meetings often result with few actionable ideas, the topics they cover can usually be dealt with over a five-minute phone call. In fact, Seth Godin goes as far as to say he won't attend meetings (at least in the typical sense) but prefers conversations where a decision can be reached. If not, meetings simply become events. Think about how much money is invested into a meeting when you have four or five employees sitting around a table for thirty minutes or an hour.

5) **Disconnect the Internet.** In a CNN survey, many respondents said they would take the Internet over sex any day. I digress. While the Internet does increase your productivity, and allows for access to information in unimaginable ways, it continues to lower the productivity of many workers. How often do you get a notification of a new email? Engaged in research and come upon a YouTube video that you just needed to watch? Had to update your Facebook or Twitter status because you just found the cutest cat picture ever? You get the point. Unplugging yourself by taking your work offline provides a level of focus that you just can't achieve online with all the potential distractions it presents. Start by implementing one of these tactics today. You'll start seeing positive results and will quickly move to implementing more of them.

Top Time-Wasting Sins

Now that I've discussed the dangers of the Internet, let me tell you about some other common time wasters you need to avoid.

Remember you are trying to be productive to get more done and enjoy the time off that can create. This is considered common sense by most, but it doesn't keep people from committing time-wasting sins each and every day.

Here are twelve of the top time wasters. How many are you making?

1) Check your Twitter stream more than twice a day.

2) Have desktop email notifications turned on.

3) Use Facebook for more than fifteen minutes a day.

4) Have windows on your computer or browser open that you are not using.

5) Have your phone vibrate or make a noise every time you get an email.

6) Be logged into Skype or other chat type program with your status set to "online."

7) Be subscribed to more blogs and newsletters than you actually read.

8) Have your phone turned on when you're writing or doing work that requires concentration and being in the zone.

9) Watch more than two hours of TV per day.

10) Working on a random list of to-dos before working on priority items.

11) Having in-person meetings when a phone meeting would deliver the same result.

12) Taking calls or replying to emails from clients, friends, and family when not urgent.

Action step: Each week select two of the twelve from above. Make a conscious goal to eliminate the two time-wasters you've selected. In less than a month, you'll see your productivity increasing. In less than two months, you'll be amazed at how much time you used to waste each day and how much more focused and productive you have become.

In today's hyper-connected world, the ability to focus becomes your superpower. We've put together a list of Productivity Boosting Tools for those who are serious about realizing their true potential.

See the list for yourself and create a true distraction-free environment at consultingsuccess.com/bookbonus

Avoid Consultant's Build Syndrome

There is another waste of time that I want to discuss. One of the biggest challenges consultants face is what I call the Consultant's Build Syndrome. Most consultants have this syndrome. They keep busy building things for their business that deliver them little to no results.

They stay home and create a new business card, brochure, website, or a fancy consultant's marketing plan.

It might take them days, weeks, or months to get these materials done.

The problem is they don't do anything with them.

People, this is a big problem! Build Syndrome is dangerous.

Here's how it usually occurs, and why it's so nasty:

1) You spend a great deal of time creating materials you'll rarely implement.

2) If you do implement them, you'll do a half-ass job of it.

3) You'll do a half-ass job of implementing because implementing is ten times harder than building.

4) You trick yourself into thinking that you're busy doing important work, when really, you're busy doing work that won't help grow your business (because you won't implement).

5) You repeat the cycle all over again.

How can you avoid this mistake?

- **Evaluate what really matters** – Here's where Pareto's Principle comes in. Also known as the 80/20 rule, the wise Italian Pareto suggested that 80 percent of our results come from 20 percent of our actions. With that in mind, take a long hard look at which 20 percent of your actions are delivering the majority of your results. Cut out the excess 80 percent of work you're doing that's giving you little to no return and put your focus where it matters most.

- **Get out of the building** – Commit to taking action. If you're going to write a report and plan to send it to 100 local businesses, do it! Success doesn't come to those who don't follow through.

- **Don't fool yourself** – Toss out the idea that keeping busy means you're on the right track. Before you start on an internal project, think hard about whether it's really going to help you build your business. If it doesn't directly help you get closer to your goals, put it on the back burner and leave room for more meaningful work.

- **Leave your comfort zone** – The number one reason for Build Syndrome is comfort. It's easy to stay at home or in the office and work away at building something. We don't have to deal with customers and the outside world. There's no rejection. It's easy. Yet it's not reality. The more you get out of your comfort zone, the more success you'll see.

Take Care of You

Think that productivity is all about the amount of work you do and how you do it? Think again. One of the keys to the consulting success I've achieved over the years is due in part to my attitude and outlook on life.

I've always been an optimistic person. When I encounter a challenge, rarely do I back down from it. One thing that has helped me to stay focused and motivated is my health.

No longer am I a star athlete (I was in my early years), but I do maintain a very healthy lifestyle. I eat good food and get lots of exercise. Five to six times a week I hit the gym. While my workouts can be short, twenty to forty minutes, they do wonders for my body, mind and business.

Exercising has many benefits:

- I come up with some of my best ideas at the gym.

- Working out provides a boost of energy.

- When I work out, I want to eat healthier.

- Exercising relieves the tightness in my neck and back that results from working at my desk.

- I keep in shape, feel good about myself and my body.

My typical routine might look like this:

1) A few stretches.
2) Running on the treadmill.
3) Longer stretches.
4) Sit-ups in three positions.
5) Shoulder pushes with weights.
6) Push-ups.
7) Bench press.
8) Bicep curls.
9) A few more core exercises.
10) Hit the hot tub.
11) Twenty laps in the pool.
12) Shower and done.

When I finish a workout like this, I feel great. My mind is clear. My confidence is high.

If you're not someone who naturally likes to go to the gym, you can make it easier on yourself by listening to music as you work out, listening to a business interview, or going for a walk.

No matter how busy you are, you really should make time to exercise. Your body, your mind, and your business will thank you for it.

It's also very important to remember to listen to yourself and give yourself a break. Literally.

Do you find yourself getting sleepy at the computer? Writer's block setting in? Does your brain feel cloudy? Feel your motivation level drop off at certain times throughout the day?

These are all common symptoms of fatigue and lack of sleep. The symptoms aren't as important as the reason why they happen, and more importantly, how to resolve them.

When sleepiness creeps in and lack of focus blurs your brain from moving forward, it can be devastating to your day and getting your work done. The cause can be anything from lack of sleep to staring at a monitor for too long to eating the wrong foods (which cause your blood sugar to spike and crash).

Luckily there is an easy solution to all of this—short breaks. I've found taking five-minute breaks throughout the day to be extremely effective in refocusing my mind and generating new ideas, not to mention helping me get more done.

You can take the five minutes anytime you need them. I usually do every hour or two. Here are a few ways I spend those five minutes:

- **Doing pushups and sit ups.** While I go to the gym daily, this break not only gets the blood moving around my body (great for energy), it also keeps me fit and pumped to get back to work.

- **Taking a walk.** Yeah, I know, five minutes isn't much time for a walk, but I'll stroll out to drop off the mail and stretch my legs.

- **Getting some fresh air.** This is similar to the above, but there's something about fresh air. Whether I hit the patio or walk a couple of blocks, fresh air does wonders.

- **Reading a magazine.** I'll pick up one of the magazines I have a subscription to, like *Inc* or *National Geographic* and read an article. This takes my mind off whatever I'm working on, and it also helps to generate new ideas.

- **Making an espresso.** This is probably more caffeine than anything else, but as I wait for the water to steam up, I get to relax my mind.

The Power of Vision

S omeone very close to me is a true visionary. They really can see into the future. Not in the fortune teller sort of way, but rather, they see trends and ideas years before they come to market.

One idea they shared with me for the health business a few years ago is just now starting to become a hot topic. If someone was to jump into this area of business right now, they'd still have many opportunities, yet imagine the person who saw this coming half a decade ago. This person isn't a one-time wonder. On several occasions now, the predictions have come true.

However, there's a big problem with all of this. All of these ideas remained just that—ideas.

The Missing Ingredient

Without taking action, investigating, developing, and implementing these ideas, nothing came of them. And I can say the same for myself. Five years ago, when I heard the health business idea, I thought, "You're right, that makes sense," but that's where I left it.

I'm sure there are countless cases like this around the world. If you have an idea or believe in something, NOW is the time to act on it.

Sure, all actions involve risk, and when you're at the front of the curve, there is always more risk involved.

Making It Work

That said, no one is twisting your arm, forcing you to make a drastic change in your life. You can still keep your job or consulting business going as you pursue your new idea. As long you're not scared of tiptoeing around late at night to get more work done or setting your alarm to go off a couple of hours earlier each day, you can find plenty of time to work on making your idea a reality.

The most you have to lose if you give it a go is some time and money. And if you go about it the right way, it'll mostly be time until you prove the potential of your idea.

What You Have to Lose

Far greater is what you have to lose if you don't give your idea a try. Some years later, you'll have that nagging feeling of regret that just doesn't go away, and you'll be constantly thinking that you should have given it a go, and what could have happened if you had.

Transforming Vision into Reality

Several years ago, I was sitting in the Japan Airlines Business Class lounge at the Tokyo/Narita airport waiting for my flight home.

Looking out over the tarmac, watching planes coming and going, tossing back a few rice cracker snacks and sipping an ice-cold Asahi beer, I thought it was a good time to reflect on the previous year and what I wanted to accomplish during the next twelve months.

I grabbed my bag and pulled out a new planning sheet that a friend of mine had sent me a couple of days earlier.

Getting Focused

Each year, like so many, I set out my resolutions and what I want to accomplish for the coming year. This year, however, I did two things that I hadn't done before, and the results surprised me: I used that new planning sheet, and I made sure to look at what I had written every day.

There I was, sitting in the lounge, filling in the sheet. I wrote about my biggest successes both in business and personally for the previous year, my biggest disappointments, and what I wanted to accomplish going forward.

The Secret Step

When I got back home, I put this sheet beside the whiteboard in my office. This might not sound like a big deal, but having it in plain sight is crucial.

I look at it every day. I review it. It gives me a lot to think about. It keeps me in check. Each time I see it, I ask myself, "Am I doing what I need to do to reach my goals?"

Four months after filling in the planning sheet, I have already achieved two of the six major goals I had for the year. And I've almost finished a third. These are big accomplishments. I don't know if I've ever come out of the gate so focused and managed to complete so much in such a short period of time.

It's Never Too Late

If you haven't taken the time to write out what your goals are, do so now. You don't need to wait for next year. It's never too late.

If you've written them down, but they are hidden away in a drawer or on a bookshelf, get them out and put them where you can see them each and every day.

This visioning thing is so powerful. It is unfortunate that people want to laugh off the idea of visioning. Or they say, "I have a plan. It's all in my head."

That won't cut it. You need to write all of this down, and put it up somewhere you can see it every day. Give it a try. I think you'll be pleasantly surprised.

Windows of Opportunity

E very day, whether you are having a good one or not, there will be windows of opportunity. You need to recognize them and then take action!

I was on the tenth floor of a building in Osaka, Japan. I'd just finished a meeting. It went well, and I was in a good mood. I got in the elevator, pushed "G" for the ground floor. The elevator stopped on the sixth floor. A guy in his late sixties got in.

Ending the Silence

As always, the elevator remained silent, but I was in a good mood. I said hello to the man and commented on the weather. It was a sunny but cold winter day. He looked at me in partial shock. I don't think he was expecting that I could speak Japanese. We got into a quick discussion and continued it outside the elevator when we reached the lobby.

The Chance

He asked me what I did. I told him about my marketing and brand consulting company—at that time I had co-founded and set up the Japan branch of the company. I asked what he did; turned out he was the president of a large import/export business. We exchanged business cards and ended up working together on some projects.

That was business I got because I took the first step. I saw a small window of opportunity to start a conversation and took it. If I had remained silent in the elevator, as is so common, I would not have landed that client.

If you don't seize your window of opportunity, you will always regret it. Robin Sharma in his book, *The Greatness Guide*, talks about the time when he saw the big movie star Harvey Keitel and wanted to go up and meet him, but he didn't. He lost the chance and regretted it.

A slight opening to meet a new prospective client. A crack that you can pass through to promote your company. An opportunity for you to do something you want, and when you don't, you later regret it.

Action

The first step to making the most of these windows of opportunity is to be open to seeing them. They are around you every day. Once you've see them, don't hesitate. Make the most of them. The worst thing that can happen is that they don't pan out the way you hoped. A door might get closed on you. So what? Going for something that you want, and hitting a roadblock or two, is far better than not going after what you want and regretting it.

Facing Challenging Times

While opening yourself up to opportunities can bring you great success, it's important to note that all consultants will face challenging times. Whether that's in the form of client issues, last minute changes, emergencies, or something else, you can get through them. There are a variety of tips that you can rely on to help guide you through handling these times professionally.

It was 7 am on a crisp winter's morning. I was going through some emails in the office. The phone rang unusually early.

As soon as I picked the phone up and heard the voice on the other end, I knew there was a problem. Thankfully, for my ear's sake, my client on the other end wasn't yelling. But he wasn't happy.

I threw my suit on, hailed a cab, and twenty minutes later I was at my client's office. He was sitting in his director's chair, smoking his cigarette. He waived for me to sit down across from him—this was going to be interesting.

It turned out that the problem my client first noticed wasn't such a big deal. In fact, through a set of coincidences, something had occurred that no one on earth could have predicted. But it happened, and I had to deal with it.

"It" was an English language advertisement that my company had created as part of a campaign for a multi-national client. That client found a similar advertisement done in Japanese by a different company using the same photo we had selected. It wasn't a competitor, and we had never seen that other ad before. Nonetheless, the client company was upset.

Within two days, the problem was resolved, but that experience taught me a great lesson in how to deal with problems.

Let's not pretend that every consulting project runs from start to finish without a hitch. Most projects hit a snag at one time or another. That's all part of being in the business.

But what should you do when a project really blows up? When something's gone wrong? When something clearly isn't right?

It's time for damage control. Let's put aside the usual, "First, figure out why the problem happened, and make sure it doesn't happen again." That makes sense, but when the pressure has caused your client's head to pop, your first action shouldn't be to think about the future. It should be to think about right now.

1) **(Wo)man Up!** - If it's your fault, admit it. Don't hide from it. Trying to put the blame on someone else or some event doesn't help. And your client will only view you in a lesser light.

2) **Be Transparent** - Explain to your client what went wrong. More importantly, tell them what you're doing to fix the situation. Everyone makes mistakes. There's no shame in admitting that you made one, if you did. Put all your cards on the table and show your client that you are holding nothing back and really do have their best interests at heart.

3) **Protect Yourself** - On the flip side if you didn't cause the problem or are being blamed for something that wasn't your fault, you need to protect yourself. Simply arguing that it wasn't you is a big mistake many people make. Come prepared. You need to reverse the odds in your favor by showing your client real proof (numbers, data, results, materials) that you've done nothing wrong.

4) **Support Them** - Regardless of whose mistake it was, you need to support your client. Clearly, they are upset and feeling stressed. Maybe the mistake has put their job on the line. Maybe they've lost a boatload of cash. Whatever it is, show your support and help them to get to the bottom of the issue and assist them in fixing it.

5) **Chill** - Seriously. Take a deep breath. This is where I messed up when I first had this experience. I got so stressed I lost sight of the other important things in life. It was a big mistake because not only did I damage my mind and body for a couple of days, but my brain was so stressed that it was clouded, which slowed down my thinking and as a result, it took longer to arrive at the solution.

To help you navigate this kind of situation, let me share with you five steps you can take to alleviate your client's unhappiness, solve the problem, and get the project train back on its tracks.

When stress hits you, and it occasionally will, do your best to put everything into perspective. What's the worst that can happen? Is it really that bad to your overall business and life? Clarifying your perspective and placing what's really important at the forefront of your mind can turn the experience into a valuable lesson. You can actually control the situation, rather than having it control you.

You Won't Succeed Alone

There is a lot you can do by yourself to benefit your business, including maximizing productivity and personal growth. As a consultant with your own business, you will often be relying on your own skills and resources to build your clientele and your success. It's just the nature of the consulting business to be self-reliant, but I want you to ask you a question.

Myth or truth? Professionals don't need help because they are professionals.

This is a common myth.

It's understandable why people fool themselves into thinking this. If you're such an expert in your area, why would you need the help of someone else? You know it all already!

That's not how it works.

Here is Eric Schmidt, Google's former CEO, on coaches:

Consulting Success

"Almost every expert in the world has a coach of some kind. I know business consultants making millions of dollars every year that can't talk highly enough about their own coaches!"

These are coaches that have coaches! Everyone can benefit from a support network. There is always something you can learn from others who have experience. That's because we all have different experiences.

Two highly skilled strategists will have slightly different skill sets, will have worked with different clients, and will have different experiences that they've each gone through.

Sometimes you'll sit down with your mentor or coach and talk to them about an issue you're having. It could be about a challenging client situation, the trouble you're having landing new clients, or dealing with a proposal you're working on. You've been having a lot of trouble with the issue. You see some solutions, but you're not sure which would be the best one to go with.

You talk with your coach and something magical happens. He explains the issues in a different way. He talks about the options from a slightly different angle. He suggests different approaches. Now, it all makes sense.

When I first started consulting, I thought I knew it all. Okay, maybe not everything, but enough that I didn't believe I needed someone else's expertise to help my consulting business grow. I was reading books on marketing, strategy, consulting, and sales more often than a steroid-stocked jock goes to the gym. I felt that was enough.

Reading is extremely empowering. The only problem is sometimes reading results in just reading; it doesn't lead to implementation and taking action.

Consulting Success

My first taste of mentorship came a few years later when I started working with one of the top consultants in my city. Actually, he hired me to help him with his marketing. It was a great experience, not only because I was getting to work with one of the smartest business growth experts I know, and not only because I was getting paid well to do it, but because I was getting an over-the-shoulder look at how this guy was running his international business.

I had first-hand access to his systems, processes, and tools. And he shared a lot of information about how he works with clients and manages his time, money, and business. I took the information and applied it to my business with great results. That was my first real taste of what a mentor could offer.

That's how a coach or mentor can help you. That's what a support network is for. You don't have to do everything yourself.

A couple of years later, I worked with and was mentored by another consultant that ran several consulting offices. Through our work together, he shared many techniques and strategies that were working for him, and that he recommended I use as well.

One day was extremely memorable. My mentor shared with me one of his secrets of pricing and fee structures. A couple of weeks later, as I met with a potential new client, I used that exact pricing structure secret. The result? It netted me an on-going project worth over $90,000.

Maybe without the information from my mentor, I still would have landed that client (I'd like to think so), but I'm pretty confident that I never would have gotten the client to accept the pricing I proposed.

Consulting Success

When looking for this kind of coaching, your mentor should:

- Have a proven-track record: You want to know that they've delivered results.

- Have existing clients. Stay away from academic consultants with no recent real-world experience.

- Offer you some sort of guarantee: It's not realistic for anyone to guarantee you results if you don't follow through, but they should take all reasonable steps to show you that they are confident you'll make the progress you're after.

- Be accessible: You don't want a mentor or coach that won't return your calls or is hard to get in touch with.

What You Need to Know

Here's the real deal. Some mentors and coaches charge a lot. Some you'll be able to work with for free or even have them pay you if they're your client (like in first example I gave). Regardless, if you can find a mentor who actually knows what they are talking about, you'd be a fool not to try and work with them. Sure, you can probably get to where you want to go without them. It'll just take you a lot longer and cost you a lot more time and money in the long run.

Yes, consultants need mentors too. You'd be wise to try and find one to help you take your consulting business to the next level. Achieving success in this business isn't easy. It becomes a lot easier when you have people there to help you. Regardless of your current level of success and experience, getting help can make all the difference.

Getting help doesn't show your lack of smarts; it demonstrates how smart you are!

Checklist: Productivity and Growth

- ☐ I have created a strategic plan that makes me matter to clients and differentiates me from competitors.

- ☐ I will set one goal a day that will benefit my business.

- ☐ I have identified my top time-wasting sins and will eliminate two each week.

- ☐ I understand the four strategies to avoid Consultant's Build Syndrome.

- ☐ I have implemented a physical health plan.

- ☐ I have put my goals down on a planning sheet and have posted it where I can see it.

- ☐ I will recognize and act on windows of opportunity.

- ☐ I understand the five steps to handle challenging situations with clients.

- ☐ I have found a qualified mentor.

Conclusion

Being a successful consultant is first and foremost about taking action. And it is critical that you are taking the right action.

This book has given you the techniques and strategies and has shared with you experiences to put you well on your way to success. It's now time to apply what you've learned.

There are too many people who have given consulting a try, yet they are consultants no longer. This has nothing to do with their level of smarts and has everything to do with their persistence, process, and approach.

I hope that you've enjoyed this journey and are excited to start applying what you've learned from these pages.

I wish you the best on your road to success! It's yours for the taking, so go and get it!

Consulting Success Coaching Program

W ould you like help to grow your consulting business?

The Consulting Success Coaching Program will help you develop skills to consistently attract ideal clients, win high-value proposals, and scale your consulting business with confidence.

How effective is your marketing system in attracting clients?

You're a great consultant. You know how to provide value for your clients and help them reach their goals. However, if you're like most of the consultants we've worked with over the last 18+ years, your challenge isn't doing the client work, it's getting more clients. And most importantly, what you want is to attract ideal high-value clients on a predictable and consistent basis.

Sustainable and Profitable Growth

Many consultants find that referrals help them to get their first few clients, but referrals from your network don't always last.

In fact, the most successful consultants don't rely on referrals. They don't "rely" on anything. They take action. They master their marketing and sales. They build a system that predictably drives new leads and ideal clients. It's a system that once planned and built (the RIGHT way) becomes one of their highest points of leverage. It's what drives the growth of their business and makes it so profitable, consistent, and sustainable.

More Clients for Your Business

We help our clients and coaching students create these systems and they consistently get results. That's exactly what the Consulting Success Coaching Program is all about. We work with a small group of dedicated consultants and teach them how to consistently attract ideal clients, earn higher fees, win more proposals, and achieve meaningful success.

To learn more about the Consulting Success Coaching Program visit
https://www.consultingsuccess.com

Praise for Consulting Success

"I realized that I was not reaching my full potential and was really just limping along with 1-2 weak prospects in my pipeline at any given time. Within 6 weeks of working with the Consulting Success team my pipeline was full and the first new clients were in place."
- **Scott Wagers**, BioSci Consulting, Belgium
Former Assistant Professor, University of Vermont College of Medicine

"My experience in the Consulting Success Coaching program has exceeded my expectations. I'm a seasoned veteran consultant for 25 years and I've been able to create a marketing platform that my business lacked and that is now in place getting me meetings with new clients."
- **Joanne Downey**, Founder, Strategy+People
Clients include Toyota, Manpower, ManuLife, Vonage, AMD

"I joined the program 2 weeks ago and have been working through my strategic offer with Michael. I met with a couple CEOs and both asked for a proposal on a next stage of work.

Within 3 days I had a confirmed project for $55k and another for $33.5k. Thank you guys for the feedback so far - let's all keep the momentum rolling!"
- **Doug Nelson**, Social Sector Board & CEO Expert
Past President BC Cancer Foundation

"Michael coached me in developing a solid marketing system that allowed me to become a full time independent consultant in just 4 months. In the last 2 months I have completely replaced the income I was receiving from my employer and I am on track to increase my income by 30% by the end of the year. Michael's methods are systematic, easy to follow, and get results."
- **Dauwn Parker**, Fundraising and CRM Consultant
Former Director City of Hope Research Center

"We had our best year ever last year, adding hundreds of thousands of dollars in new revenue, and I'm very excited for the growth we'll experience this year! I've worked as part of large consulting companies and consulted for some of the world's biggest businesses. When it came to growing my own consulting business this coaching program was a clear fit. I've invested a significant amount of money to work with Michael and his team and I continue to. It's been a great investment."
- **Jitendra Badiani**, CEO,
Focused Improvement Consulting, Toronto
Former Director, PwC and Dunkin' Brand

"I was running a successful agency and wanted to shift from doing all the work for our clients to providing strategic advice. With Michael's help and the team at Consulting Success that's exactly what we achieved within a few short months. We've now sold several new advisory packages and have 5 more

proposals in the works. Michael's suggestions pushed me beyond what I thought was possible. We're getting 3x more leads than before, we have a lead generation process in place that works consistently, and we're working with world-class clients as advisors in a leveraged way. Working with Consulting Success is an investment, but it's a very worthwhile one."
- **Andrew Kucheriavy**, UXMC, CEO, Intechnic
Clients include BMO, Blue Cross, Camping World

"Since joining the Consulting Success program I have been able to increase the fees on my proposals and increase the long-term value of my client engagements. I've just loved getting really specific feedback it's been great."
- **Kristen Gallagher**, Founder, Edify
Clients include AWS Elemental, Puppet, FlightGlobal

"We landed our largest project to date with the help and guidance from Michael and the team at Consulting Success. Our revenue has consistently grown, our pipeline is full of opportunities and things keep improving month over month."
- **James S.** Corporate Financial Consultant, New Zealand

"Michael's ideas and expertise have served my company very well! We hired Michael to help us define revenue paths and approaches for our new consultancy--from strategic to tactical. He helped us define and articulate the company's direction, strengths, goals, and leverage points. Michael's expertise has provided us with an understanding of how to gain more customers and communicate a unique value proposition that addresses their problems. As a result, we have expanded our client base! He will make your company more successful! Hire him!!"

Consulting Success

- **Gary Kyle**, Federal Contracting Consultant
Former Principal Booz Allen Hamilton

"I've doubled my business in less than 12 weeks. Consulting Success helped me to re-package my offerings and improve my pricing structures which lead to a 40% increase in my fees and I've already landed 2 new projects at my new rate and I'm confident many more to come."
- **Sonaya Williams**, Sonaya Williams Group
Former Senior Analyst, TD Ameritrade

"As a successful entrepreneur recently transitioning into a consulting practice, joining the Consulting Success Coaching program and working with Sam and Michael was the best decision I could have made. I have gone through several coaching programs and mastermind groups but Consulting Success was different for me. It's the first program that provided a focused, linear path to success with a clear, detailed process, accountability, tremendous group support and specific tools to ensure your success. Beyond that, you have complete access to Sam and Michael who clearly have the best interests of their clients in mind at all times and continue to find new ways to provide additional value. It's refreshing to work with a group of highly successful individuals who have already been where you're going and who can provide real world advice and support."
- **Josh Canova**, CEO Pow Wow Growth Strategies
Former founder Detour Films, clients included Reebok, Pfizer, Toyota, Ad Council

"I decided to use Consulting Success's services in an effort to grow my business. I had things going rather well, but knew that I could do better. Michael helped me in finding the

unused potential that I had and leverage that in a short time span. Within 2 months, I've been able to increase the size of the deals as well as my pipeline and to have a clean plan on how to move my business."
- **Tsahi Levent-levi**, WebRTC Consultant
Former CTO Radvision

"I decided to level up again by investing in the coaching program. I was able to land new client contracts which easily was more than 3x my investment. I anticipate making so much more throughout the year with the tools that I invested in. It's a no brainer... hire Michael as a coach and stop wasting time and money."
- **Damien Wilpitz**, Lab Research Consultant
Former Research Manager Harvard Medical School

"Mike helps you to focus on the right things and build stronger value. Since being in the program, I have significantly expanded my reach and increased my sales by 45%. Most importantly, he has given me great advice structuring more profitable offerings which also add better results for my clients."
- **Kate Caldecott**, Founder, Kate Caldecott & Associates
Clients include City of Melbourne and Australia Post

"I've landed 11 new clients during the program. I didn't know what I was getting into when I jumped on a call to learn more about the program, but I'm so glad I did. I sincerely appreciate everything that I've received in terms of support. I've increased my billings exponentially."
- **Donna Bates**, Founder, On Point Strategy, Australia
Former Marketing and PR Director, Australian Army

"The Program has netted me well in excess of the coaching fees within weeks of beginning. Michael has provided invaluable coaching and insight that has really helped me to develop my business. He's 'been there, done that' and the experience really pays off. Top notch!"
- **Jeff Griffiths**, Partner, Calgary, Canada
Griffiths Sheppard Consulting Group

"I joined the program to zero in on my ideal client so that I could get my value proposition, fee structure, and offerings focused. My investment in the program started paying off quickly, and within weeks I landed a new client and have real clarity that will help me in the months and years to come using what I have learned."
- **Scott Gillespie**, Agronomy Consultant
Clients work with McCain, Cavendish, Lamb Weston, & Frito Lay

"With Michael by our side, pushing us to rethink some of the fundamentals we were overlooking and tweak even just small things about our process, we beat our revenue goal by 25%. And that's after Michael recommended we double it on our first call with him."
- **Shane Reiser**, Partner, Your Ideas Are Terrible
Former Director at Dwolla

Get a Free 47-Page Consulting Blueprint

At the time of printing, Consulting Success is offering a FREE 47-page Consulting Blueprint. You'll learn:

- How to develop a clear specialization that showcases your expertise

- Steps to attract ideal consulting clients

- Tips to improve your proposals and win more deals

- How to effectively structure your consulting offers

- And much more...

For instant and free access visit:

www.consultingsuccess.com/blueprint

About the Author

Michael Zipursky is an entrepreneur, coach to consultants, and CEO of ConsultingSuccess.com. He is a leading authority on marketing for independent consultants and consulting businesses, business growth, and pricing strategies. He has advised organizations like Financial Times, Dow Jones, RBC, Omron, Sumitomo and helped Panasonic launch new products into global markets, but more importantly, he's helped over 300 consultants from around the world in over 50 industries add six and seven figures to their annual revenues.

Michael is the author of the Amazon Bestseller *The Elite Consulting Mind*. His work has been featured in *Forbes*, *Entrepreneur*, *MarketingProfs*, *Maclean's*, Institute of Management Consultants USA, Canadian Association of Management Consultants, and Chartered Management Institute in the UK.

Made in the USA
Middletown, DE
18 December 2021